—— FORMING ——

INTENTIONAL
DISCIPLES

—FORMING—
INTENTIONAL
DISCIPLES

The Path to Knowing and Following Jesus

Sherry A. Weddell

OUR SUNDAY VISITOR PUBLISHING DIVISION
OUR SUNDAY VISITOR, INC.
HUNTINGTON, INDIANA 46750

TABLE OF CONTENTS

Acknowledgments

Writing this book would have been impossible without a host of men and women who have inspired, challenged, encouraged, and vetted me. Many thanks to:

- The tens of thousands of Catholics around the world who have generously shared their experiences of being used by God in the course of the Called & Gifted discernment process. You have opened an incredible window on the world of *living* Catholicism and given us a tantalizing glimpse of the river of God's redeeming grace that flows ceaselessly into our world through the assent and cooperation of "ordinary" Catholics.
- The 1,600 parish and diocesan leaders who have shared both their struggles and hard-won wisdom during various versions of our Making Disciples evangelization training over the past eight years.
- Our Catherine of Siena Institute staff, teachers, donors, collaborators, and champions who made the adventure of writing a book in five months — while spending two of those months on the road — possible!
- The wonderful disciples and apostles who agreed to be interviewed or shared their evangelical wisdom with me in other ways, including:

    Nancy Arkin, Rod Bennett, Dennis Branconier, Nina Butorac, Father Chas Canoy, Father James Conlon, Katherine Coolidge, David Curp, Bobbi Dominick, Barbara Elliott, Deacon Dan Foley,

Father Ed Fride, Francisco "Paco" Gavrilides, Lisa Hills, Father Dennis Howard, Father Gregory Jensen, Corinne Lopez, Father John Maduri, Dr. Ralph Martin, Carol McGee, Daniel Moore, Scott Moyer, Father Edward Pelrine, Tom Peterson, Ellen Piper, Craig Pohl, Sara Silberger, Gaurav Shroff, Keith Strohm, Tina Terrant, Jane Twilliger, and Dr. Peter Williamson.

- Dr. Carole Brown, who let me read her insightful dissertation on evangelization in the thought of Blessed John Paul II.
- Mark Gray, at the Center for Applied Research in the Apostolate (CARA), for clarifying some of CARA's figures for me.
- Roz Dieterich, who offered warm hospitality and her considerable organizational gifts to a near stranger, and who, with her husband, Henry, shared their experience of life at Christ the King Parish.
- The input and prayers of my band of Facebook friends, especially Tim Ferguson, who originally suggested the title, and Woodeene Koenig-Bricker for her editorial insight and support.
- The members of the San Fernando Region Evangelization Committee, who, under the leadership of Bishop Gerald Wilkerson, have been a catalyst of a remarkable evangelization vision in the Archdiocese of Los Angeles: Edward Arno, Katie Dawson, Ben Decenario, Yvonne Garcia, Frank Luciano, Sally Meyers, and Bobby Vidal.
- Sherry, who listened and prayed me through it all, and Jim, whose computer mastery triumphs over my technology anti-charism every time.

- My wonderful Evangelization Brain-Trust and other honored collaborators who ensured that this book would be rich in reality-based evangelical wisdom. God bless you. You know who you are!
- My dear friend Mark Shea, who shared so much of his extensive writing and editorial wisdom with me. You have thanked me in print in the past for helping you with a few of your books. I still owe you one.
- Cindy Cavnar, my patient editor, who managed the task of walking a first-time "editee" through a rather daunting process with grace and good humor.
- Father Michael Fones, O.P., who was not only my co-Director but my closest collaborator during the voyage of discovery that has been our work in parish-centered evangelization. God bless you, Father Mike, for your own discipleship; your spiritual openness, energy, and incredible work ethic; your sense of adventure and humor; and your great generosity and kindness to all of us at the Institute and to me personally. You kept me on my toes. I never knew what you might do next when we were teaching, but none of this would have been possible without you.

INTRODUCTION

In 1997, Father Michael Sweeney, O.P., and I founded the Catherine of Siena Institute, a ministry of the Western Dominican Province. Our mission is to equip parishes to form lay apostles. Our working assumption at that time was that most Catholics just needed solid apostolic formation in order to discern and answer God's call. We used the Called & Gifted discernment process I had developed as a way to introduce Catholics to the idea that they were apostles with a mission by virtue of their baptism. Over 65,000 Catholics — priests, seminarians, religious, and lay — have gone through the Called & Gifted process to date, in hundreds of parishes in 105 dioceses on 5 continents.

In many ways, however, this book began to take shape in 1993, when, as a volunteer, I taught the very first Called & Gifted Workshop to twenty handpicked people in Seattle. From the beginning, I offered what I call "gifts interviews": private, one-hour, one-on-one sessions that help individuals recognize consistent patterns of giftedness. I would listen as Catholics told their stories of being used by God for others. In the early days, I did a considerable amount of nodding and making encouraging sounds, since I had very little idea of what I was supposed to be listening for. But I learned through experience and have since trained thousands of pastoral leaders to conduct these gifts discernment interviews.

One of these gifts interviews was remarkable for the fact that it drew the Institute into direct involvement with evangelization. In 2004, Dominican Father Mike Fones and I were teaching in a large Canadian city, where a pastor had asked us to interview a few of his leaders. I subsequently found myself listening to a woman who was president of the local Catholic women's group, but I wasn't getting anywhere. Her stories were so vague that I wasn't hearing any evidence of how God might be using her. Since charisms do not manifest until one's faith becomes personal, I reasoned that if she could tell me about a spiritual turning point in her life, I would be able to focus on the years since that turning point. So I asked her a question that I had never asked before: *Could you briefly describe to me your lived relationship with God to this point in your life?*

After thinking carefully for a few moments, she responded briskly, "I don't have a relationship with God." Her answer stunned me. My first thoughts were, "That's not possible. You're a leader in the parish. You wouldn't do that without *some* kind of relationship with God. I must have asked the wrong question." So I spent the rest of the hour approaching the issue of relationship with God from every perspective I could think of. By the end of the interview, I realized that she had accurately described her spiritual reality in the first place. While God had a relationship with her (or she would not exist!), she did not have a conscious relationship with God. No wonder she struggled to discern her charisms! Her parish involvement was devoid of spiritual motivation.

I thought long and hard about that interview. I later told Father Mike, "That's the most amazing interview I've ever done. Maybe we should ask that question more often." And so the two of us started routinely asking the "Describe your lived relationship with God" question in the course of our gifts interviews. The answers we received — from hundreds of ordinary Catholics and parish leaders all over the world — were consistently revealing and often astounding. And we have learned a great deal more by listening to over 1,600 diocesan and parish leaders from 60 dioceses who have attended our evangelization seminar, Making Disciples, over the past eight years.

What have we learned? We learned that there is a chasm the size of the Grand Canyon between the Church's sophisticated theology of the lay apostolate and the *lived* spiritual experience of the majority of our people. And this chasm has a name: *discipleship*. We learned that the majority of even "active" American Catholics are still at an early, essentially passive stage of spiritual development. We learned that our first need at the parish level isn't catechetical. Rather, our fundamental problem is that most of our people are not yet disciples. They will never be apostles until they have begun to follow Jesus Christ in the midst of his Church.

We learned that at the parochial level, we have accepted this chasm between the Church's teaching and Catholics' lived relationship with God as *normative*, and this has shaped our community culture, our pastoral assumptions, and our pastoral practices with devastating results. We discovered, to our surprise and dismay, that many pastoral leaders do not even possess a conceptual category for discipleship. As long as this holds true, the theology of the laity and the Church's teaching on social justice and evangelization will remain beautiful ideals that are, practically speaking, dead letters for the vast majority of Catholics.

Finally, we learned that God, in his providence, has already given us all the resources we need — theological, pastoral, and practical — to move into the new century empowered to meet this challenge and the host of other challenges that face us. This book, like all the work of the Catherine of Siena Institute, is ordered toward helping the Church accomplish just that.

Almost all of the Institute's work has been done within the parochial system, and not with ecclesial movements or other specialized groups. I have tremendous admiration for these movements, but they ultimately touch, at most, only 1 to 2 percent of the Church's membership. The only contact that most Catholics have with the Church is through their local parish or mission, which is why we have focused on equipping parishes. If life at the parish level changes, the life of the whole Church will change.

At the seminary- and graduate-school level, there is currently very little formation in practical evangelization available for Catholics, especially as regards effective evangelization at the parish level in the postmodern West. Most of the evangelizing parishes that we have encountered are only two to five years into the process. The parish that we have worked with the longest has only been evangelizing for fifteen years. I have only been listening to Catholics tell me their stories for eighteen years. We are all pioneers in this area, and we are all on a steep learning curve.

The good news is that we have met many amazing, creative pastoral leaders who are deliberately calling Catholic men and women to make the journey to intentional discipleship, and are beginning to see the extraordinary fruit and cultural changes that follow. Whatever wisdom and insight this book contains comes from the tens of thousands of Catholic men and women around the world who have honored us with their stories. I am also drawing upon the experiences of a network of pioneering evangelizers and pastoral collaborators.

I can only share in this book what we know from the Church's teaching and have witnessed God do among his people to this point. That means that there are many gaps in our understanding, and that there are many questions we have yet to answer. But I believe that there is a definite trajectory to this learning experience, and that the implications are very exciting and hopeful.

CHAPTER 1

God Has No Grandchildren

"A sower went out to sow. And as he sowed, some seeds fell along the path, and the birds came and devoured them. Other seeds fell on rocky ground, where they had not much soil, and immediately they sprang up, since they had no depth of soil, but when the sun rose they were scorched; and since they had no root they withered away. Other seeds fell upon thorns, and the thorns grew up and choked them. Other seeds fell on good soil and brought forth grain, some a hundredfold, some sixty, some thirty."

MATTHEW 13:3–8

I had only been Catholic a few months when a priest first explained to me that my peers who were leaving the Church would return when they got married or had children. This vigorous man had been ordained before the Second Vatican Council and is still active today. He retained a serene confidence in the irresistible drawing power of a Catholic childhood and of the sacraments. A young person might leave but (he was confident) would always come back in the end, captured by G. K. Chesterton's "unseen hook and an invisible line which is long enough to let him wander to the ends of the world, and still to bring him back with a twitch upon the thread."[1]

Twenty years later, however, national studies have revealed that those who leave the Church do *not*, by and large, return. They usually go elsewhere or stop practicing their faith altogether. But besides showing the inadequacy of our current efforts, the available research also gives us unexpected reasons to hope and many clues about how to most effectively focus our evangelical efforts. In this first chapter, we will take an extended look at the big picture that emerges from the research. That will set the stage for the focus of the following eleven chapters: exploring how we can stem the tide of Catholic losses and better meet the spiritual needs of the millions who are searching for faith at this very moment.

CLIMATE CHANGE

We must first grapple with the reality that we live in an era when religious identity is not stable but remarkably fluid. Although the focus of this book is primarily the Catholic Church in the United States, this religious fluidity is a global phenomenon and certainly not limited to Catholics. According to the *Atlas of Global Christianity*, 61.2 million people were added to the worldwide Christian fold in a single year — 2010.[2] Of these, 16 million were converts *to*

---

[1]   G. K. Chesterton, *The Innocence of Father Brown, Centennial Edition* (Seattle: CreateSpace, 2010), p. 44.

[2]   Todd M. Johnson, Kenneth R. Ross, eds., *Atlas of Global Christianity: 1910–2010* (Edinburgh, Scotland: Edinburgh University Press, 2009), p. 61.

Christianity from some other background. *In the Catholic Church, specifically, an average of 41,000 new Catholics were born into or entered the universal Church on every single day of 2010.*[3]

Christianity: Conversions and Defections, Worldwide, 2010
* 16 million converted
  — 43,800 converted every day
* 11.6 million left
  — 31,780 left every day

Christianity: Births and Deaths Worldwide, 2010
* 45.2 million born into Christian families
* 21.7 million Christians died

Christianity's Net Gain, 2010
* 27.8 million[4]

Unfortunately, the movement goes both ways. Some 11.6 million Christians *left* Christianity during 2010. Add the number of those who chose to leave to the number of those who converted, and we see that an amazing number of people — roughly 27.6 million — moved deliberately in or out of the Christian world in a single year. *That's 5 million more than the entire population of Australia.* The conversions are taking place mostly in the global South, and the defections mostly

---

[3] "Presentation of Pontifical Yearbook 2012," Vatican Information Service, March 12, 2012 (online at http://visnews-en.blogspot.com/2012/03/presentation-of-pontifical-yearbook.html, as of May 8, 2012).

[4] Johnson and Ross, *Atlas of Global Christianity: 1910–2010*, p. 61.

in the West. Still, after births and conversions are weighed against deaths and defections, there was an average of 76,000 additional Christians every single day of the year.[5]

The spiritual winds blow both ways in our postmodern world: *into* and *out* of the Church. Our spiritual climate provides us with real opportunities (of which more later) and very definite threats if we do not adjust our evangelizing, catechetical, and pastoral practice to the unique challenges of the times in which we live.

What is true of the world is especially true in the United States.

> The ["U.S. Religious Landscape"] survey [of 2008] finds that constant movement characterizes the American religious marketplace, as every major religious group is simultaneously gaining and losing adherents. Those that are growing as a result of religious change are simply gaining new members at a faster rate than they are losing members. Conversely, those that are declining in number because of religious change simply are not attracting enough new members to offset the number of adherents who are leaving those particular faiths.[6]

5   Ibid.

6   Pew Research Center's Forum on Religion & Public Life, "U.S. Religious Landscape Survey," 2008 (online at http://religions.pewforum.org/, as of May 8, 2012). Two surveys conducted by the Pew Research Center's Forum on Religion & Public Life served as this book's major source for analysis of religious life in the United States. The surveys are (1) the "U.S. Religious Landscape Survey," conducted in 2007 and released in 2008, and (2) "Faith in Flux," conducted in 2008 and released in 2009. The analysis of the data is the author's.

According to the Pew Forum on Religion & Public Life's recent studies of religious change, approximately 53 percent of American adults have left the faith of their childhood at some point; 9 percent have left and returned.

LIVING IN THE LAND OF "NONE"

The Pew "U.S. Religious Landscape Survey" of 2008 shows the fastest-growing religious demographic in the United States to be "unaffiliated" (aka "nones"). These are the one in six American adults who say they are not affiliated with any religious group or tradition.

A family gathering in Seattle — my hometown — provided a vivid experience of what this spiritual climate can look like. I was blogging in the early morning at a local coffee shop, which was trying to look as if it was frozen in the 1940s. It might have succeeded except for the industrial-strength espresso, computers, Wi-Fi, and piles of alternative newspapers. The place was very Seattle: a soft granola exterior with a hard-edged, twenty-first-century underbelly.

But even more quintessential was the "what-to-do-in-Seattle" magazine, which ended with an essay about how the Emerald City was the heart of "None Land." The article's point was that when Seattle inhabitants were asked what religious tradition they identify with, 60 percent answered "None." As a native daughter, it was enough to make me spill my skinny Irish cream latte. You know that practical agnosticism has won when it is loudly proclaimed as part of a city's identity in a publication written for tourists.

MY RELIGION? "NONE"

- 16.1% adults are "unaffiliated"
  — 1/3 "just haven't found the right religion"
- 24% of 18- to 29-year-olds are "unaffiliated"

It is essential that we grasp that "unaffiliated" today is *not* necessarily akin to "unbelief." Only a quarter of American "nones" chose the label "atheist" or "agnostic" to describe their spiritual beliefs; three-quarters said that they were "nothing in particular." The "U.S. Religious Landscape Survey" divided the latter into two distinct subgroups:

- The "religious unaffiliated" included those who said that religion was important or very important to them even though they didn't identify with any particular religious tradition. They often turned out to be believers who didn't regard themselves as belonging anywhere.
- The "secular unaffiliated" comprised those who declared that religion had little or no importance for them.

"RELIGIOUS UNAFFILIATED"

Americans for whom religion is important or very important but who are not affiliated with any religious tradition or community:

- 94% believe in God or a "universal spirit"
- 49% believe in a personal God
- 30% are formal members of religious congregations
- 11% attend religious services weekly; 46% attend at least yearly

- 17% are involved in congregational activities at least once a month
- 65% pray at least weekly outside of religious services; 44% pray daily
- 78% believe miracles happen today
- 46% have talked to others about their ideas of God

What surprised the Pew surveyors was how religiously active "unaffiliated" people could be. Thirty percent were formal members of a congregation. How can one consider oneself "unaffiliated" and yet be formally enrolled in a congregation? Although practicing Catholics don't typically have a mental category for "I'm a member of St. Anthony Parish, but I'm not a Catholic," a sizable number of twenty-first-century "nones" do. Appreciating this important distinction is to confront the very heart of our new spiritual climate.

But we can glean from this report the good news that *many* unaffiliated Americans are still open to a religious identity of some kind. One-third say they would join a religion, but they have not yet found the right one. Even more significantly, 54 percent of American adults who were raised without faith later chose one as an adult. So whether they were raised in a faith or not, chances are that twenty-first-century Americans will revisit the whole issue as adults and choose for themselves.

WHO'S AT MASS?

What this means for the Catholic Church in America is that on any given weekend, our parishes host significant numbers of spiritually open people who do not claim a Catholic identity — even though some may have received the sacraments of initiation. We are hardwired to assume that if we spy someone at Mass, he or she is Catholic. If that was ever the case, it certainly is not true now. "Nones" and all sorts of spiritual seekers routinely float in and out of our sanctuaries for reasons of their own. They are not hostile to the Church; indeed, they are often open in remarkable ways.

An excellent example is the amusing experience of a woman who blogs under the *nom de plume* "Robin of Berkeley." Robin describes her first experience of attending a church service, a Christmas Eve Mass:

> I searched the Internet and found a large Catholic church the next town over. My plan: come early and sit inconspicuously in the back row.... For one, I didn't want to make a fool of myself. I'd never been to church, and I had no idea what to do.... A woman smiled and introduced herself as Cathy. She asked me whether the other priest was feeling better. The following conversation ensued:
>
> *Me:* I don't know. I've never been to this church before.
> *Cathy:* Oh, really? Where do you usually worship?
> Me (stammering): Well. Actually, I've never been to a church before.
> *Cathy (puzzled):* Oh. Are you here to see one of the children perform?
> *Me:* No. (I want to give her a clear explanation, but given that I don't know why I'm here, my mind goes blank.)
> *Cathy (thinking deeply):* So you've never been in a church but decided to come here on Christmas Eve?

Me: Yes. (Her explanation was simpler than the one I would have given: "I'm a cultural Jew who's never been to a temple, and then I practiced Buddhism for twenty years, but that left out the God part.... Now I have all these beautiful Christians in my life, so I decided to attend a Mass, and the Berkeley Episcopalians didn't want me, so here I am.")

Robin's immersion in things Catholic took a startling turn when she was asked to hand out Christmas-carol sheets. She looked for another usher to see what she should do and discovered to her horror that she was the only one. When she finally managed to escape that job, she took refuge in the vestibule by a pretty fountain and then discovered that a line of patient people was forming behind her. She wrote: "Note to self: blocking the holy water is another church no-no." Despite these missteps, Robin found that

it was a magical night. Beyond the music and pageantry, what moved me the most was being with hundreds of people who loved God. Maybe some were questioning his presence or feeling abandoned. But they showed up, and that's half of life. It was a stirring night for this wandering Jew who has traveled from east to west, from Left to Right. As the Sufi poet Hafiz wrote, "This moment in time God has carved a place for you," and sitting in the sanctuary, I felt that place.[7]

---

[7] Online at www.americanthinker.com/2009/12/power_to_the_conservative _peop.html, as of May 8, 2012.

Of course, a Robin of Berkeley who wanders in under her own steam is hardly the whole story of those religiously unaffiliated who frequent our churches. Two groups, self-identified Catholics and "religiously unaffiliated" respondents to the Pew poll — and I find this particularly striking — were more similar in their responses than any other pair of "faith" groups. This similarity is likely no accident. Although there are indeed many religiously unaffiliated like Robin coming from a background completely outside the Christian tradition, there are also a huge number of people wandering back into our parishes whose religious journey began when they were babies at that pretty fountain Robin was blocking. The number of "former" Catholics in the United States is so large that there is a high probability that many "religious nones" are former Catholics who retain an idiosyncratic mix of Catholic and non-Catholic beliefs and practices.

Ebb and Flow

A study of the Pew statistics concerning adults *who were raised Catholic* is sobering. *Only 30 percent of Americans who were raised Catholic are still "practicing"* — meaning they attend Mass at least once a month. Roughly half of these are at Mass on a given weekend. Another 38 percent hold on to their Catholic identity but seldom or never attend Mass. The final 32 percent — almost a third of all adults who were raised Catholic in the United States — no longer consider themselves to be Catholic at all: 3 percent are now part of a non-Christian faith; 14 percent consider themselves unaffiliated; 15 percent are now part of some Protestant faith tradition.[8]

When it comes to tracing the journeys of former Catholics, we have to keep in mind the important differences between major strands of Protestant Christianity, especially between evangelical Protestantism and mainline Protestantism. This distinction is important because the lion's share of Catholics who enter the Protestant world become evangelicals.

> Churches within the evangelical Protestant tradition share certain religious beliefs (such as the conviction that personal acceptance of Jesus Christ is the only way to salvation), practices (such as an emphasis on bringing other people to the faith) and origins (including separatist movements against established religious institutions). In contrast, churches in the mainline Protestant tradition share other doctrines (such as a less exclusionary view of salvation), practices (such as a strong emphasis on social reform) and origins (such as long-established religious institutions).[9]

What this religious fluidity means for the Catholic Church in the United States is striking. Fully 10 percent of all adults in America are ex-Catholics, while 2.6 percent

---

[8] These figures were extrapolated by the author to incorporate not only those who currently claim a Catholic identity but all adults who were Catholic at some point in their lives. This would include the 10 percent of American adults who are former Catholics.

[9] Pew, "U.S. Religious Landscape Survey," 2008.

are converts to the Church. In other words, *nearly four times as many adults have left as have entered the Church.* The life-blood of new members being transfused into the Church is a steady trickle, while the blood being lost is a hemorrhage. Lately, even the trickle is slowing down. The annual number of adult converts received into the Church dropped over 35 percent between 2000 and 2009.[10]

COMING AND GOING

Catholic adults in the U.S.
- 2.6% have entered Catholicism
  - 178,533 adults entered in 2000
  - 115,194 adults entered in 2009
- 10.1% have left Catholicism

Protestant adults in the U.S.
- 8.4% have entered Protestantism
- 11.0% have left Protestantism

"Unaffiliated" or "None" adults in the U.S.
- 12.7% have entered "None Land"
- 3.9% have left "None Land"

The flow of Americans into Protestantism, as a whole, is more than three times larger than the movement into Catholicism. Nearly five times as many become "unaffiliated" as enter the Catholic Church. The only religious group in

---

[10] United States Conference of Catholic Bishops (USCCB), *The Catholic Church in the United States at a Glance*, 2009 (online at http://old.usccb.org/comm/catholic-church-statistics.shtml, as of May 8, 2012).

the United States that matches the growth rate of "nones" is non-denominational evangelicals.

An old saying captures our situation as Catholics vividly: *God has no grandchildren.* Protestants, particularly evangelicals, are highly attuned to the spiritual mobility of postmodern Americans and constantly consider how to reach out to them. One of the deepest convictions of evangelical culture is that every person, whether raised inside a Christian tradition or not, has a personal decision to make about whether he or she will live as a disciple of Jesus Christ. It should therefore not surprise us that 49 percent of American adults who are now evangelicals were raised outside evangelicalism, and 18 percent outside Protestantism altogether.

CONVERSION AND AMERICAN RELIGIOUS IDENTITY

	Convert	Raised as Member
Catholic	11 %	89 %
Jewish	15 %	85 %
Orthodox	23 %	77 %
Mormon	26 %	74 %
Muslim	40 %	60 %
Evangelical	49 %	51 %
Buddhist	73 %	27 %
Unaffiliated	79 %	21 %

In contrast, Catholic pastoral practice still assumes that religious identity is largely inherited and stable throughout one's life span. So firm is our sense of Catholicism as a "faith into which one is born" that many Catholics are surprised to discover that millions of their brothers and sisters are converts. What we have taken as normative is, in fact, the far end of the "religious bell curve." Catholicism has the second-highest percentage of "native" members of any major faith in the United States. All other U.S. faiths, with the exception of Hinduism, have a higher percentage of converts, including Judaism, Orthodoxy, Islam, mainline Protestantism, and Buddhism.

GOING SOMEWHERE AND GOING NOWHERE

Where do Catholics go when they leave? There are two basic paths or tracks taken by the vast majority. The 15 percent who eventually become Protestant (Track A) — which includes the 9 percent who join evangelical communities — are motivated differently than the 14 percent who become "nones" or "unaffiliated" (Track B).

Catholics who become Protestants say that their strongest reason for doing so was "that my spiritual needs were not being met." Interestingly, cradle Protestants who join a *different* kind of Protestant faith, as well as those "nones" who were raised without a faith but chose one as an adult, also told Pew researchers that this was their primary reason for changing faiths. Hence, all three groups share a similar basic motivation for their spiritual journey: "My spiritual needs were not being met."

BECOMING PROTESTANT: WHY I LEFT CATHOLICISM

- 71%   "My spiritual needs were not being met."
- 70%   "I found a religion I liked more."
- 21%   Sexual-abuse scandal
- 3%   Separation or divorce

BECOMING PROTESTANT:
WHY I JOINED A PROTESTANT FAITH

- 81%   Enjoyed new faith's services and worship
- 62%   Felt called by God

TRACK A: BECOMING PROTESTANT

The most important reason that former Catholics who end up as Protestants gave for *leaving* the Church was, as indicated above, "My spiritual needs were not being met." Catholics who became *evangelical* Protestants were even more likely to state that this was their primary reason for leaving (78 percent). The second most important reason for leaving was "I found a religion I liked more." Very few Catholics-turned-Protestant left because of separation or divorce. And even though 21 percent said that they left because of the clergy abuse scandal, it was a distant third as a motivation for leaving.

Speaking of that scandal, a telling 2011 study by Dr. Daniel Hungerman at the University of Notre Dame found that 2 million Catholics left the Church (roughly 3 percent) and 3 billion dollars was given to non-Catholic causes as a result of the sex scandal. Surprising beneficiaries were Baptist congregations; these made the most gains in membership and income.[11] Twenty-three percent of the 2 million Catholics who left because of the scandal joined non-main-

---

[11] "Catholic Sex-Abuse Crisis Boon for Baptists, Economist Dan Hungerman Shows," University of Notre Dame, *College of Arts & Letters News*, November 11, 2011 (online at al.nd.edu/news/27380-catholic-sex-abuse-crisis-boon-for-baptists-new-research-shows/, as of May 8, 2012).

line Protestant congregations, while 51 percent became "unaffiliated." Only 2 percent became Episcopalians.[12]

So much for why these people left the Catholic Church. When asked why they chose to *join* a Protestant faith, the overwhelming majority responded that they enjoyed their new faith's services and worship. In a response that many believing Catholics will find both incredible and infuriating, 62 percent of all who became Protestant and 74 percent of those who became evangelical said that they "felt called by God."

As frustrating as it can be for Catholics to hear this, it is critical that we listen carefully when spiritual seekers give us their reasons for changing faiths. It is all too easy to project our own passionately held theological and ecclesial convictions upon people who are motivated by entirely different questions and concerns. I cannot tell you how many times I have heard intelligent Catholics casually dismiss evangelical worship as mere "entertainment" while showing no understanding of what motivated millions of their former Catholic brothers and sisters to embrace that form of worship in the first place.

I recently worked with a group of pastors and pastoral leaders at a diocesan evangelization seminar. I asked, "What have the lapsed Catholics that you know told you about why they left?" I received a broad spectrum of familiar answers: people didn't agree with certain teachings; they didn't believe anymore; they were looking for community; they felt the desire to be "fed," and so forth. Then one woman said, "Evangelical mega-church services are enter-

12 Motoko Rich, "Affiliation Before and After Scandal," *New York Times*, November 14, 2011.

tainment. They just want entertainment," and a number of heads nodded in agreement.

So I asked her, "Is that the language that your friends actually used? Did they say that they wanted to be entertained? Did they actually use the word *entertainment*? Our goal here is to understand what motivates lapsed Catholics, so we need to listen to the language they actually use."

The woman looked puzzled by my question, which I had to repeat to the whole group: "Have you actually heard former Catholics tell you that they have started attending evangelical churches in order to be 'entertained'?" Slowly the truth dawned on us. The "entertainment" thesis reflects our Catholic insider judgments about what *we presume* must have motivated those who have left the Catholic Church for evangelical communities. But none of us had ever heard a living former Catholic use that language.

Certainly no former Catholic that I have met in the evangelical world has ever talked about a desire for "entertainment" as a motivation for ceasing to attend Mass. In fact, there is a staggering gap between the dominant "story line" that you hear from former Catholics whom you meet in the evangelical world (which is usually some variation on "I never met Jesus in a living way as a Catholic") and the judgments that many Catholic pastoral leaders blithely make about why they left.

Track B: Becoming a "None"

In sharp contrast to those who convert to some form of Protestantism, unaffiliated ex-Catholics — those on Track

B — are more likely to say that they simply drifted away. We all know Catholics who do not accept or believe all of the Church's teaching but still practice their faith. But for those who leave the Church for "None Land," unbelief becomes a powerful motivation to leave Christianity altogether.

BECOMING UNAFFILIATED: WHY I LEFT CATHOLICISM
(Many respondents gave more than one answer.)

- 71%   "Just gradually drifted away."
- 65%   "Stopped believing in the religion's teachings."
- 27%   Sexual-abuse scandal
- 3%   Separation or divorce

BECOMING UNAFFILIATED: WHY I BECAME A "NONE"

- 42%   Don't believe in God/most religious teachings
- 33%   Have not found the right religion

The majority of "nones," those who become unaffiliated, said that they stopped believing certain Church teachings, including those on abortion, homosexuality, birth control, divorce, and remarriage. In contrast, Catholics who become Protestant (Track A) are much less likely to say they left for those reasons. For instance, only 16 percent said that the Church's teaching on birth control was an issue for them.

Less than a third of Catholics who became "nones" said that their faith was very strong as a child. When asked why they chose to become unaffiliated, 42 percent responded that they "just do not believe in God and most religious teachings." However, one-third of them made it clear that their spiritual journey was not over and that they "just have not yet found the right religion for them."

The concerns of Catholics who leave and remain un-affiliated are concerns that many Catholics recognize and debate endlessly. Catholics across the spectrum have strong opinions on how the Church's teachings on homosexuality and birth control, for instance, relate to the exodus and what should be done about it. And so it is striking that the different motivations of the 15 percent who eventually become Protestant — those who are still Christians — seem much more difficult for us to grasp and effectively respond to.

Young Adults and Religious Change

Religious change has long been young-adult territory. *Catholics who leave, leave early.* This is especially true today. Nearly half of cradle Catholics who become "unaffiliated" are gone by age eighteen. Nearly 80 percent are gone and 71 percent have already taken on an "unaffiliated" identity by their early twenties.

LEAVING EARLY

Catholics who became "unaffiliated"
- 79% left Catholicism by age twenty-three
  - 48% left by age eighteen
  - 71% "unaffiliated" by age twenty-three

Catholics who became Protestant:
- 66% left Catholicism by age twenty-three
  - 39% were Protestant by age twenty-three
  - Another 41% were Protestant by age thirty-five
  - 60% become evangelicals

In contrast, Catholics who depart for Protestantism move more slowly. Yet two-thirds are gone by age twenty-three. They often spend some years in spiritual transition before joining a Protestant faith in their late twenties or early thirties. Only 39 percent have become Protestant by age twenty-three, and another 41 percent become Protestant by age thirty-five. The majority join evangelical faiths. Perhaps Catholics-turned-Protestant move more slowly because the majority are on a personal spiritual quest.

WHEN WHAT WORKED BEFORE
DOESN'T WORK ANYMORE

Since the late sixteenth and early seventeenth centuries, the Catholic retention strategy has been (a) childhood catechesis and (b) sacramental initiation. Four hundred years ago, CCD (Confraternity of Christian Doctrine) and the Catholic school system were cutting-edge responses to the crisis of the Protestant Reformation. Setting out to give every Catholic child a solid catechetical background was an extraordinary vision that had never before been attempted. The endeavor was deeply influenced by a Renaissance optimism about the power of education. The assumption was that a carefully nurtured religious identity acquired in childhood would endure throughout life. The Jesuit motto said it all: "Give me a child until he is seven, and I will give you the man."

But the evidence suggests that what worked in the seventeenth century does not work in the twenty-first. Pew researchers found that attending CCD, youth groups, and even Catholic high schools made little or no difference in whether or not an American Catholic teen ended up staying Catholic, becoming Protestant, or leaving to become "unaffiliated."

RAISED CATHOLIC, "VERY STRONG FAITH"

	Child	Teen	Adult
Still Catholic	46 %	34 %	46 %
Now Protestant	36 %	22 %	71 %
Now Unaffiliated	30 %	12 %	12 %

RAISED CATHOLIC, RELIGIOUS ATTENDANCE

	Child	Teen	Adult
Still Catholic	86 %	69 %	42 %
Now Protestant	79 %	60 %	63 %
Now Unaffiliated	74 %	44 %	2 %

As we can see in the above table, the best predictor of adult attendance at religious services is strong *adult* faith. The significantly higher worship attendance of Catholics who become Protestant makes sense in terms of the very dramatic growth in strong personal faith between their teen (22 percent) and adult (71 percent) years. It is the adult's spiritual journey — building upon his or her experience as a child and teenager — that is most likely to translate into lifelong faith and consistent religious practice. Indeed, one of the most ironic twists in our current predicament is this: *In the early twenty-first century, among Americans raised Catholic, becoming Protestant is the best guarantee of stable church attendance as an adult.*

Weekly attendance of those who remain Catholic drops significantly in adulthood. Most of those who will become "unaffiliated" attend Mass as children, but their personal faith drops to a very low level as teens and never recovers.

WON'T THE SACRAMENTS BRING THEM BACK?

Our pastoral practice still operates on the presumption that although most Catholic teens vanish after Confirmation, they will find their way back when they are ready to get married and especially when they have children. One huge problem with this paradigm is that Catholic marriage rates are, in fact, plummeting. The number of marriages celebrated in the Church decreased dramatically, by nearly 60 percent, between 1972 and 2010, while the U.S. Catholic population increased by almost 17 million.[13]

CATHOLIC MARRIAGE

1972:	415,487 Catholics got married
	8.6 marriages/1,000 Catholics
	79% adult Catholics were married
	69% young-adult Catholics were married
2010:	168,400 Catholics got married
	2.6 marriages/1,000 Catholics
	53% adult Catholics were married
	38% young-adult Catholics were married[14]

---

[13] Mark Gray, "Exclusive Analysis: National Catholic Marriage Rate Plummets," *Our Sunday Visitor*, June 26, 2011.

[14] Ibid.

There are many factors in play. First of all, a much smaller percentage of Catholics chooses to marry at all. The percentage of Catholics who said that they are married dropped 26 percent between 1972 and 2010. Among young adults (ages eighteen to forty), the percentage of married Catholics dropped over 30 percent during the same period.[15] According to the 2007 survey "Marriage in the Catholic Church," by the Center for Applied Research in the Apostolate (CARA),[16] 24 percent of never-married Catholics thought it unlikely that they would ever marry. In addition, young Catholics who are still getting married are not necessarily doing so in the Church. Forty percent of married Generation X and Millennial Catholics were not married in the Church.[17]

The 35 percent drop in adults entering the Church through the Rite of Christian Initiation of Adults (RCIA) since 2000 may well be related to the dramatic drop in Catholic marriages. The RCIA is primarily a young-adult venture. Forty-eight percent of adults entering the Church through the RCIA do so by age twenty-nine, and 64 percent do so by age thirty-nine.[18] According to the U.S. bishops' 2000 study of the RCIA, the majority of those going through the RCIA were young adults in their thirties

---

[15] Ibid.

[16] Mark M. Gray, Ph.D., Paul M. Perl, Ph.D., Tricia C. Bruce, Ph.D., *Marriage in the Catholic Church*, Center for Applied Research in the Apostolate (CARA), 2007, p. 106.

[17] Ibid., p. 69.

[18] Mark M. Gray, Ph.D., and Paul M. Perl, Ph.D., *Sacraments Today: Belief and Practice Among U.S. Catholics*, Center for Applied Research in the Apostolate (CARA), 2008, p. 25.

who attended for marriage and family reasons. Most had a Catholic spouse or were planning to marry a Catholic.[19] But if fewer young-adult Catholics are married or planning on getting married, fewer spouses and engaged men and women will be entering the Church.

In any case, the number of young Catholic adults practicing their faith has also dropped. In the 2007 marriage study, CARA published some disturbing figures about Mass attendance.

ATTENDING SUNDAY MASS, 2007

By Generations

Builders	Ages 65+	45%
Boomers	Ages 47–64	20%
Gen X	Ages 26–46	13%
Millennials	Ages 18–25	10%[20]

Take a moment to consider the implications. More than 50 percent of Catholic adults are now either Gen Xers or Millennials, and that percentage will only grow. Both

---

[19] United States Conference of Catholic Bishops (USCCB), *Journey to the Fullness of Life*, Executive Summary, 2000.

[20] CARA, *Marriage in the Catholic Church*, 2007, p. 31. CARA has adopted a method of research that eliminates most of the "inflation" of figures that results when a respondent naturally wants to appear good in the eyes of the questioner. When actual head counts are taken, the resulting attendance statistics can be as little as half of what is self-reported. That is why CARA attendance figures are smaller than those gathered by Pew Forum, although both show the same trajectory.

groups are teetering on the brink of single-digit weekly Mass attendance. If younger Catholics are not going to Mass or getting married in the Church, why would they bother to raise their children in the faith? We can no longer depend upon rites of passage or cultural, peer, or familial pressure to bring the majority back.

If this trend does not change, in ten years it will cease to matter that we have a priest shortage. The Builders will be largely gone, the Boomers retiring, and our institutions — parishes and schools — will be emptying at an incredible rate. Sacramental *practice* will plummet at a rate that will make the post-Vatican II era look good, and the Church's financial support will vanish like Bernie Madoff's investment portfolio. So let's be clear: *In the twenty-first century, cultural Catholicism is dead as a retention strategy, because God has no grandchildren. In the twenty-first century, we have to foster intentional Catholicism rather than cultural Catholicism.*

Religious Change: It's Not Just for Anglos

The same dynamics that affect the larger Catholic community are also evident among Hispanics. According to the 2010 U.S. Census, there are 50.5 million Hispanics in the U.S.[21] The Pew Forum's 2007 study of the religious faith of Hispanic Americans found that 68 percent of Hispanic adults identify as Catholics, 8 percent are "unaffiliated,"

---

[21] "Census Data Shows Hispanic Boom," *The Christian Science Monitor,* March 24, 2011.

and 1 percent are non-Christian.[22] The rest belong to other Christian faiths. The "American Religious Identification Survey" found that, when considering only the 31 million adult Hispanics, the number of Catholics had slipped to 60 percent, and Catholic "nones" were 12 percent.[23] Although the numbers are slightly different, the overall trajectory of all recent studies of Hispanic faith is the same.

HISPANICS AND FAITH, 2007

- 68% Catholic
- 15% Evangelical Protestant
- 8% Unaffiliated
- 5% Mainline Protestant
- 3% Jehovah's Witness/Mormon
- 1% Non-Christian

According to Pew researchers, 13 percent of Hispanics have converted from Catholicism to something else. The other shoe has yet to drop: *21 percent of Hispanics who are still Catholic told Pew surveyors that they were open to changing faiths, and 5 percent didn't know or refused to answer the question.* Many may be in the period of dissatisfaction and

---

[22] Unless otherwise noted, data regarding Latinos and American life is taken from the Pew Hispanic Center's survey "Changing Faiths: Latinos and the Transformation of American Religion," conducted in 2006 and released in 2007. The survey was conducted in collaboration with the Pew Research Center's Forum on Religion & Public Life. The analysis is the author's.

[23] *U.S. Latino Religious Identification 1990-2008: Growth, Diversity & Transformation,* "American Religious Identification Survey," 2008, Highlights.

struggle that tends to precede departure from the Catholic Church. Religious identity is fluid for Hispanic young adults as well, and becoming more so. A 2010 Associated Press-Univision poll found that only 55 percent of young Hispanics, ages 18–29, claimed to be Catholic.[24]

It is fascinating to learn that Hispanics who convert to another Christian faith are motivated much like Catholics who become Protestant, and to a greater degree. Eighty-three percent of Hispanic converts to *any* Christian faith and 90 percent of Hispanic converts to evangelicalism say they were seeking a more direct, personal relationship with God. This intense concern for direct, personal relationship with God makes sense when we consider that the majority of both Hispanic Catholics and Hispanic Protestants are charismatic in spirituality.

The liturgy is a factor in the decision to stay or to leave for many. Sixty-one percent of Hispanics who leave Catholicism say that the liturgy is not "lively and exciting," although "lively and exciting" is never defined. Thirty-six percent of Hispanic converts from Catholicism to Protestantism say that the liturgy was actually a factor in their becoming Protestant. On the other hand, 71 percent of those Hispanics who stay Catholic say that they find the liturgy to be "lively and exciting."

Another contributing factor in changing Hispanic religious identity is their assimilation into the majority culture. Hispanics are much more likely to be non-Catholic if they are born in the United States. Similarly, if their dominant

---

[24] "Poll: Young Hispanics Less Likely to Be Catholic," *USA Today*, August 10, 2010.

language is English, they are twice as likely to be non-Catholic. If they are second- or third-generation residents of the United States, Hispanics are more likely to convert to Protestantism or leave the Church.

MULTITUDES IN THE VALLEY OF DECISION

Underneath all the sobering realities we have been considering lie some surprising and hopeful opportunities. For instance, the "U.S. Religious Landscape Survey" found that the majority of American adults who change from their childhood faith do so in a series of steps rather than a single giant leap. This holds true for former Catholics too. Very few people wake up one morning and decide, "I think I'll become a Baptist today." All the evidence is that people feel dissatisfied and consider leaving for a couple of years before actually taking the first step, and that the majority pass through two or three religious changes before settling into a new spiritual home. Most people have mixed feelings about leaving the faith of their childhood. They are unsure of leaving and unsure of where to go after they leave. In other words, changes of faith are, for most people, *a journey and a search*, not an instant, simple, and painless abandonment of belief.

The truth is that at this very moment, millions of Americans, including many ex-Catholics, are open to the faith of Jesus Christ and his Church. Consider those who we know who are either actively searching or at least passively scanning the horizon for spiritual alternatives:

- Those who were raised without a faith and who are exploring their options.

- Those who have left a childhood faith but "haven't found the right faith yet."
- The millions of "religious unaffiliated" who know religion is important, pray regularly, and wander in and out of our congregations.
- Catholics who have left the faith but have not yet adopted another religious identity and are searching.
- Dissatisfied Catholics who haven't left but are considering doing so.

These people are already seeking. Our job is to reach out deliberately and intentionally to help them find the pearl of great price.

It's All About Relationship

When Pew researchers asked American adults a series of questions about the kind of God they believed in, a startling pattern emerged: *Nearly a third of self-identified Catholics believe in an impersonal God.*

I had always blithely assumed that when people said that they believed in God, they meant a personal God. What other kind of God is there? Not so. Only 60 percent of Catholics believe in a *personal* God. Twenty-nine percent said that God is an "impersonal force." Eight percent responded that God was "other," or "both" personal and impersonal, and 1 percent didn't believe in God at all.

It is especially sobering to learn that when Pew surveyors asked the question, "Which comes closest to your view of God: God is a person with whom people can have a relationship, or God is an impersonal force?" only 48 percent of Catholics were *absolutely certain* that the God they believed in was a God with whom they could have a personal relationship.

So it should be clear that retaining a Catholic identity does not mean that someone necessarily believes in the God at the heart of Catholicism. How much of our faith can make sense to millions of Catholics when the bedrock foundation — belief in a personal God who loves us — is not in place?

I noticed something in the Pew results that made me stop and look again: for younger Catholics, the level of attendance at worship services is directly correlated with the *certainty* that it is possible to have a *personal* relationship with God. This correlation is *not* true for older Catholics, those sixty-nine years of age and above. Of the older generation, 62 percent attend Mass, while only 57 percent are certain that they can have a relationship with God.

As the Pew report put it, Catholics have the biggest "generation gap" of any religious community in the United States. Sixty-two percent of Catholics sixty-five and older in 2008 said they attended Mass every week, while only 34 percent of Millennials did so. For younger Catholics who came of age after the cultural tsunami of postmodernity swept through the West in the 1960s, *Mass attendance is always lower than, and goes up and down with, the percentage of those who are certain that it is possible to have a personal relationship with God.*

	Personal Relationship With God and Mass	Attendance
All:	48%	42%
Men:	43%	36%
Women:	53%	45%
18–29:	40%	34%
30–49:	46%	36%
50–64:	54%	42%

This trend held true across the three age groups studied and across gender. The younger the group, the lower the number who were certain that God was personal and who said that they went to Mass every week. Only 40 percent of Catholics eighteen to twenty-nine were certain that it is possible to have a personal relationship with God, and only 34 percent of them reported being at Mass on a weekly basis.

The same correlation between certainty that a personal relationship with God is possible and attendance at church seems to hold true outside the Catholic world. Seventy-three percent of all evangelicals are confident that you can have a personal relationship with God, and weekly attendance reflects that. For instance, 71 percent of evangelical Millennials believe you can have a personal relationship with God, and 54 percent of them attend church every week. The attendance gap in evangelical circles between sixty-five-plus elders (65 percent) and twenty-somethings (54 percent) is less than a third of that found among Catholics.

Where does all this leave us? Certainly, one of the most fundamental challenges facing our Church is this: *The majority of adult Catholics are not even certain that a personal relationship with God is possible.* In short, statistical reality bears out this prophetic passage from Pope John Paul II's *Catechesi Tradendae* (On Catechesis in Our Time): It is possible for baptized Catholics to be "still without any explicit personal attachment to Jesus Christ; they only have the *capacity* to believe placed within them by Baptism and the presence of the Holy Spirit."[25]

So we live in a time of immense challenge and immense opportunity. Millions of American adults are seeking a religious identity and are at least potentially open to the Catholic faith. At the same time, huge numbers of self-identified Catholics are not certain that a personal relationship with God is even possible, and their actions reflect it. The majority of Catholics in the United States are *sacramentalized* but not *evangelized.* They do not know that an explicit, personal attachment to Christ — personal discipleship — is normative Catholicism as taught by the apostles and reiterated time and time again by the popes, councils, and saints of the Church.

A few years ago I was having breakfast with an archdiocesan vocation director. On impulse I asked him, "What percentage of the men you work with — men discerning a possible call to the priesthood — are already disciples?"

---

[25] Pope John Paul II, *Catechesi Tradendae* (On Catechesis in Our Tme), 19 (online at www.vatican.va/holy_father/john_paul_ii/apost_exhortations/documents/hf_jp-ii_exh_16101979_catechesi-tradendae_en.html, as of May 8, 2012; emphasis added).

His answer was immediate: "None."

"Why do you think that is?"

He was very clear: "They don't know how. No one has ever talked to them about it."

How can a man discern a call to the priesthood if he has not yet experienced the relationship that is at the heart of the faith? How can the men and women he shepherds fulfill St. Paul's call to "grow up in every way into him who is the head, into Christ" (Ephesians 4:15) if neither he nor they believe that a personal relationship with, and following, Jesus Christ in the midst of his Church is, indeed, normal Catholic life?

To wrestle with the numerous questions and trends brought forth in this chapter, we have to explore what it means to be a disciple of Jesus Christ in the midst of his Church.

CHAPTER 2

We Don't Know
What Normal Is

Jesus Christ did not come to suffer and die so that he could make "cultural Catholics."

ARCHBISHOP JOSÉ GOMEZ OF LOS ANGELES[1]

When I visited Most Precious Blood Parish in Brooklyn, I felt as if I had walked onto a movie set. Here were the gestures, the accents, and the living feel of a world that I had seen depicted hundreds of times in films and on television. Now I was encountering the real thing and, with it, a unique and deeply rooted form of Catholic culture.

One of my guides was Nancy Arkin, a lifelong New Yorker who has worked in pastoral ministry in the Diocese of Brooklyn for twenty years. For the past three years, Nancy has served as coordinator of adult faith formation at Most Precious Blood, which is located in an area that was majority Italian for generations. But the tide has turned. The Italians have moved out in droves, and their place has been taken by Chinese and Russian immigrants who are not Catholic. Like most parishes in the area, Most Precious

---

[1] Jeff Ziegler, "The Coming Latino Catholic Majority," *Catholic World Report*, December 1, 2011.

Blood's membership has dropped nearly 80 percent from its height in the 1960s, and the majority who attend are elderly. Many in the neighborhood now have no Christian background at all.

Father Maduri, who grew up in the parish next door, became pastor in 2009 and responded in a remarkable way. He sized up the situation quickly: Either the human community had to be rebuilt or the parish would close. Since the traditional Catholic population was leaving the area, he would focus on making disciples of the unbaptized and apostles of the baptized. To do that, he had to introduce a core of his committed parishioners to ideas that were rather new. As Nancy put it:

> The whole idea of the Holy Spirit — that God was actively engaged in a relationship with [people] and calling them to live it out, that they were his instrument so that others would know the Gospel — was quite unfamiliar. The people I've met here — this was completely new to them. Everyone says it is new. It was all Greek to them.... I am amazed that they are so receptive and responsive.

As a beginning, Father Maduri brought in some enthusiastic young evangelists who are part of a Catholic group called "Dirty Vagabonds," which specializes in the personal evangelization of urban youth. These recent graduates of the Franciscan University of Steubenville sport lots of conversation-starting tattoos, live very simply, and spend their afternoons with the kids in the neighborhood and in the projects nearby.

In 2012, the parish will begin reaching out to the huge number of Chinese immigrants in the area. When I realized that I was in the midst of a group of lifelong New York-Italian Catholics who were planning to learn Chinese in order to evangelize their new neighbors who have no Christian background, I felt like Dorothy in *The Wizard of Oz*: "Toto, I've a feeling we're not in Kansas anymore!"

How rare is this? As the late Avery Cardinal Dulles noted:

> Asked whether spreading the faith was a high priority of their parishes, 75 percent of conservative Protestant congregations and 57 percent of African-American congregations responded affirmatively, whereas only 6 percent of Catholic parishes did the same. Asked whether they sponsored local evangelistic activities, 39 percent of conservative Protestant congregations and 16 percent of African-American congregations responded positively as compared with only 3 percent of Catholic parishes. [2]

Father Maduri and Nancy are wrestling with a whole new kind of mission and pastoral ministry in Brooklyn. Their situation is being repeated in parishes and dioceses all over the Western world, which is why Pope Benedict has called for a Synod on the New Evangelization to be held in Rome in 2012.

---

[2] The statistics cited are from a study by Nancy T. Ammerman, *Pillars of Faith* (Berkeley: University of California Press, 2005), tables on pp. 117, 134, cited by Cardinal Dulles in the forward to the book by Timothy E. Byerley, *The Great Commission: Models of Evangelization in American Catholicism* (New York: Paulist Press, 2008), p. ix.

TRANSMITTING THE FAITH: THE *LINEAMENTA*

The *Lineamenta*, or a set of guidelines for discussion issued in preparation for the synod, is not a compilation of high-level abstractions. Rather, the guidelines form a serious meditation on where we actually are in the post-Christian West in terms of our ability to transmit a living, personal Catholic faith to future generations. Certain words pepper the *Lineamenta*: *disciple, personal, encounter, change, missionary, experience, transmit, proclaim, Jesus, live,* and *Gospel.* It is equally telling that the phrase *Catholic identity* is nowhere to be found.

The emphasis on *transmit* is crucial, because transmitting the faith is an organic, whole-person, whole-life concept that goes far beyond instruction in facts or doctrines. This holistic approach is clearly very much on the minds of those who drafted the *Lineamenta*:

> Transmitting the faith means to create in every place and time the conditions for this personal encounter of individuals with Jesus Christ. The faith-encounter with the person of Jesus Christ is a relationship with him, "remembering him" (in the Eucharist) and, through the grace of the Spirit, having in us the mind of Jesus Christ. Pope Benedict XVI stated: "Being Christian is not the result of an ethical choice or a lofty idea, but the encounter with an event, a person, which gives life a new horizon and a decisive direction...."

> This personal encounter allows individuals to share in the Son's relationship with his Father and to ex-

perience the power of the Spirit. The aim of transmitting the faith and the goal of evangelization is to bring us "through him [Christ] in one Spirit to the Father" (Eph 2:18).[3]

The discussion begins by recognizing that transmission of the Catholic faith is not just passing on an inherited religious identity. Genuine Catholic identity flows *from* the experience of discipleship. As the *Lineamenta* notes:

> *What is not believed or lived cannot be transmitted....*
> The Gospel can only be transmitted on the basis of "being" with Jesus and living with Jesus the experience of the Father, in the Spirit; and, in a corresponding way, of "feeling" compelled to proclaim and share what is lived as a good and something positive and beautiful.[4]

If a living relationship with Christ and, therefore, his Father and the Holy Spirit, does not exist, we have not succeeded in "transmitting" the faith. The faith has not been transmitted unless the Person and the relationship at the center of the faith have been transmitted. And we can't successfully transmit the relationship at the center of the faith unless we ourselves consciously participate in that relationship.

---

[3] Lineamenta of the 2012 Synod Assembly, 11 (available online at http://www.vatican.va/roman_curia/synod/documents/rc_synod_doc_20110202_lineamenta-xiii-assembly_en.html, as of May 8, 2012).

[4] Ibid., 12, emphasis added.

THREE SPIRITUAL JOURNEYS

Normative Catholicism involves three concurrent spiritual journeys that, in practice, are often treated as separate:

1. The personal interior journey of a lived relationship with Christ resulting in intentional discipleship.
2. The ecclesial journey into the Church through reception of the sacraments of initiation.
3. The journey of active practice (as evidenced by receiving the sacraments, attending Mass, and participating in the life and mission of the Christian community).

Father Mike Fones and I experienced the separation of these three journeys in a conversation we once had with some seminarians. We were talking about the experience of a young Catholic friend who had just gone through a dramatic conversion. When I used the term "intentional disciple" to describe our friend, one seminarian responded, "Oh! You mean he has taken up his Catholic identity."

Ideally, discipleship and Catholic identity would always be one and the same. Every Catholic would be making all three journeys — to be a conscious disciple of Jesus Christ, a fully initiated Catholic, and an active parishioner — as an integrated whole. But what is often meant by the term "Catholic identity" is simply regarding oneself as Catholic and attending Mass with reasonable regularity. In this view, there is no need to inquire into the nature of one's lived relationship with God. In short, many Catholics think one needn't ask about the *first* journey if the *second* and *third* journeys are in place.

The problem with this view is aptly described by Father Damian Ference, a member of the formation faculty at Borromeo Seminary in Wickliffe, Ohio:

> All too often those of us in positions of Church leadership presume that all the folks in the pews on Sundays, all the children in our grade schools, high schools and PSR programs, all the kids in our youth groups, all the men in our Men's Clubs and all the women in our Women's Guilds, and all the members of our RCIA team are already disciples. Many are not. (The same can be said of staffs and faculties of Catholic institutions.) Our people may be very active in the programs of our parishes, schools and institutions, but unfortunately, such participation does not qualify for discipleship.[5]

The common working assumption that we encounter is that personal discipleship is a kind of optional spiritual enrichment for the exceptionally pious or spiritually gifted. This makes perfect sense if we remember the realities outlined in chapter 1. *Personal discipleship will inevitably be treated as a kind of optional accessory in a Catholic community where less than half are confident that they can have a personal relationship with God and nearly 30 percent don't believe in a personal God at all.*[6]

---

[5] Father Damien Ference, "Why Vocation Programs Don't Work," *Homiletic and Pastoral Review*, February 2011.
[6] Pew, "U.S. Religious Landscape Survey."

THE CULTURE OF "DON'T ASK, DON'T TELL"

As we listened to the spiritual experiences of tens of thousands of Catholics, we began to grasp that many, if not a majority of, Catholics don't know what "normal" Christianity looks like. I believe that one reason for this is the selective silence about the call to discipleship that pervades many parishes. Catholics have come to regard it as normal and deeply Catholic to *not* talk about the first journey — their relationship with God — except in confession or spiritual direction. This attitude is so pervasive in Catholic communities that we have started to call it the culture of "Don't Ask, Don't Tell."

Unfortunately, most of us aren't spiritual geniuses. If nobody around us ever talks about a given idea, we are no more likely to think of it spontaneously than we are to suddenly invent a new primary color. To the extent that we don't *talk* explicitly with one another about discipleship, we make it very, very difficult for most Catholics to *think* about discipleship.

Sara Silberger, New York mother of four and poet, experienced this when she became Catholic. Sara was raised by a nonpracticing Catholic mother and a Jewish father and had never practiced any faith herself. A mystical experience triggered an intense exploration of Catholicism that led twenty-eight-year-old Sara to be received into the Church at Easter 2010. Sara told me that she was surprised and puzzled by the fact that lifelong Catholics were so uncomfortable talking about their relationship with God:

> About six weeks into the [RCIA] program, I met with Sister and told her that I thought maybe I was

missing something, because we didn't seem to be talking much about getting to know God or Jesus. I didn't feel like I had a good understanding of who Jesus was to me. I assumed that this was because I was coming from a non-Christian background and everyone else already "got it." ... I had to go out and ask Catholic friends to talk to me about these things, one-on-one. Some were willing to tell me, sort of — but all but one of them also got visibly upset first and didn't know why I'd want to know about their experiences. I had a sense that they resented being asked.

One of our most surprising discoveries has been *how many Catholics don't even know that this personal, interior journey exists.* A high-level, cradle-Catholic leader on the West Coast acknowledged to me recently that the very idea of a personal relationship with God was still new to him. The possibility had only dawned upon him for the first time a few years ago, when his parish started offering evangelizing retreats.

Widespread neglect of the interior journey of discipleship has unintentionally fostered an immense chasm between what the Church teaches is normal and what many Catholics in the pews have learned to regard as normal. Many lifelong Catholics have never seen personal discipleship lived overtly or talked about in an explicit manner in their family or parish. It is difficult to believe in and live something that you have never heard anyone else talk about or seen anyone else live. It is also very difficult to openly hold a minority opinion or speak of a minority experience in the midst of a group that does not understand.

The Spiral of Silence is a well-known communication theory originally proposed by political scientist Elisabeth Noelle-Neumann. In her research, Noelle-Neumann found that people are less likely to voice an opinion on a topic if they believe they are in the minority, because most people fear isolation from the majority. One of the crucial points of the Spiral of Silence theory is that people are constantly observing the behaviors of those around them, to see which behaviors gain approval and which receive disapproval from the majority. Recent research in neurology has begun to uncover the physiology behind this behavior:

> According to researcher Vasily Klucharev of Erasmus University in the Netherlands ... when people hold an opinion differing from others in a group, their brains produce an error signal.

> "If you make an error, it means that something [wrong is going on]. And, whenever we experience an error, it means this error signal pushes us to change behavior," Klucharev said. "And, we see it looks like we quite automatically produce this signal when our opinion is quite different from other people.

> "The researcher examined two brain areas," said Klucharev. "The first, a zone of the brain popularly called the 'oops area,' becomes extra active signaling an error; while the 'reward area' is less active, making people think they made a mistake."[7]

---

[7] Jessica Berman, "Brain Mapping Social Conformity," *The Cutting Edge*, January 19, 2009 (online at www.thecuttingedgenews.com/index.php?ar ticle=1041&pageid=&pagename=, as of May 8, 2012).

Existing parish culture often reinforces a Spiral of Silence about one's relationship with God. This Spiral of Silence does not usually become explicit until it is challenged, but it can strangle evangelization, especially as it is reinforced today by a religion-doesn't-belong-in-the-public-square cultural norm. It is essential for us to grasp that the cultural pressure, both *inside* and *outside* the average American parish, is often *against* the overt expression of discipleship. The two overlapping cultural norms — one secular and one ecclesial — intimidate men and women who seek to live as Catholic disciples of Jesus Christ. In order to counter that pressure and "live out loud" as intentional Catholics, they absolutely need strong interpersonal, communal support.

It Is Normal

In the fall of 1993, a group of young-adult friends in Seattle got together to create a support group for lay Catholics. We called our little community the "Nameless Lay Group" (NLG) because we couldn't think of a good name. Over time we became a multi-parish, multigenerational gathering of twenty- to sixty-somethings, married and single, half cradle Catholics and half converts. What we had in common was a hunger for a truly supportive Catholic community centered on personal discipleship. Former community members, now living around the country, still talk wistfully about those days in Seattle, because the humble NLG remains the most powerful experience of Christian community that any of us have experienced as Catholics.

Our leadership team drew up a vision-and-values statement we called the "*It is Normals*":

Our Vision
That we would be a Catholic community that nurtures the faith and gifts of lay Catholics, enabling them to become effective, committed disciples of Jesus Christ who have discerned and are living out their God-given mission in life.

Our Values
1. It is *NORMAL* for lay Catholics to have a living, growing love relationship with God.
2. It is *NORMAL* for lay Catholics to be excited Christian activists.
3. It is *NORMAL* for lay Catholics to be knowledgeable about their faith, the Scriptures, the doctrinal and moral teachings of the Church, and the history of the Church.
4. It is *NORMAL* for lay Catholics to know what their charisms of service are and to be using them effectively in the fulfillment of their vocation or call in life.
5. It is *NORMAL* for lay Catholics to know that they have a vocation/mission in life (primarily in the secular world) given to them by God. It is *NORMAL* for lay Catholics to be actively engaged in discerning and living this vocation.
6. It is *NORMAL* for lay Catholics to have the fellowship of other committed lay Catholics available to them, to encourage, nurture, and discern as they attempt to follow Jesus.

7. It is *NORMAL* for the local parish to function consciously as a house of formation for
lay Catholics, which enables and empowers lay
Catholics to do #1–6 above.

The impact of a small but intentional gathering of disciples can be surprising. Our little group was able to help
frustrated Catholics stay in as well as help Protestants enter
the Church — including a whole family in New Zealand
via the Internet. Victor, the then-Baptist husband of one
NLG member, summed up his feelings this way: "You are
the first Catholics that I knew were real Christians." The
good news is that Victor has since entered the Church.

We knew that *none* of our seven values were "normal" in
the sense of something that you could routinely expect to
find practiced in the average parish. But we also knew that
they were "normal" in the sense that the Church understood
them to be part of *normative* Catholicism. The Church has
reiterated time and again that

the "good news" is directed to stirring a person to a
conversion of heart and life and a clinging to Jesus
Christ as Lord and Savior; to disposing a person to
receive Baptism and the Eucharist and to strength-
en a person in the prospect and realization of new
life according to the Spirit.[8]

---

8   Pope John Paul II, *Christifideles Laici* (Apostolic Exhortation on the Vocation and the Mission of the Lay Faithful in the Church and in the
World), 33 (online at http://www.vatican.va/holy_father/john_paul_ii/
apost_exhortations/documents/hf_jp-ii_exh_30121988_christifideles-
laici_en.html, as of May 8, 2012).

But it is clear that large numbers of baptized Catholics have not experienced this relationship. In the course of our Making Disciples seminars since 2004, we have asked hundreds of diocesan and parish leaders from sixty dioceses throughout the English-speaking world this question: *What percentage of your parishioners, would you estimate, are intentional disciples?* To our astonishment, we have received the same answer over and over: "Five percent." Remember, these leaders were referring to *approximately 5 percent of those who darken the doors of our parishes,* because those are the people they knew. (Catholics who rarely or never attend Mass seldom interact with pastoral staff.)

Clearly, this wasn't a scientific survey, but is it likely that the educated guesses of this many experienced leaders from this many dioceses are wildly off the mark? Is it possible that only a single-digit percentage of the more-or-less "active" Catholics in our parishes are intentional disciples? Ralph Martin speaks directly to this reality:

> This means recognizing that we can no longer presume that those coming for the sacraments still understand what it means to be a Catholic or are even committed to such. Nor can we presume that they even know who Christ is and have made a commitment to him as savior and Lord. Nor can we presume that what they are seeking when they come for the sacraments is what indeed the sacraments are intended to effect.[9]

---

[9]   Ralph Martin, "The Post Christendom Sacramental Crisis: The Wisdom of St. Thomas Aquinas." Forthcoming, *Nova et Vetera.*

As we listened to Catholics talk about their spiritual journey, we began to realize that many assumed there were two basic spiritual "tracks": "ordinary Catholic" and "saint." We discovered that many Catholics, including some pastoral leaders attending our seminars on evangelization, have no imaginative category for one who is an intentional follower of Jesus "on the way" but not yet a saint. There is a strong tendency to account for those who try to live as disciples by labeling them "extraordinary," either positively, as called to priestly or religious life, or negatively, as pretenders to sanctity.

This tendency has been the experience of Daniel Moore, a young man we met in Colorado Springs. After years of serious drug addiction, Daniel experienced a dramatic conversion and was instantly freed from his addiction. Daniel was so passionate about his new discipleship that many people, including priests, told him that he should consider the priesthood. The problem was that Daniel was a construction worker who had barely squeaked through high school and had never read a book until after his conversion. It was very unlikely that he would make it through six years of graduate-level philosophy and theology. In an odd sort of way, people weren't seeing Daniel the man at all. They just didn't know what else to suggest to a young, single man who had had such a powerful encounter with God.

Another tendency is to dismiss an enthusiastic disciple as a spiritual pretender or zealot. Overtly enthusiastic disciples strike many Catholics as arrogant, extreme, overly emotional, and elitist. I have heard disciples who live their faith "out loud" dismissed as Protestants dozens of times, even when they are cradle Catholics who have never left the Church or ever been involved with a Protestant community.

A West Coast director of religious education (DRE) told me recently that his parish's former RCIA director didn't want people on her RCIA team who had gone through significant conversions: "They are too extreme. They are 'Protestant' because they are too 'on fire.'"

This Catholic discomfort with overt spiritual passion is another expression of the Spiral of Silence. Daniel Moore has experienced this also. A mutual priest-friend was put off when, in a burst of enthusiasm, Daniel urged him, "Let's be saints!" He said his first impulse was to wish Daniel would calm down and stop sounding so "Protestant." *Who* did Daniel think he was?

Eventually, my priest-friend recognized that his real issue was not that Daniel was too extreme. He realized that the fire of his own discipleship, the spark that had fueled his priestly vocation, had burned low. Daniel's passion illuminated his own spiritual state.

What Is Discipleship?

The Spiral of Silence must end if a vibrant culture of discipleship is to be fostered at the parish level. That means recognizing, first of all, that discipleship is *never* unconscious. What do I mean?

A couple of years ago a friend was being trained as a catechist in a large archdiocese. She was solemnly informed in a class on spiritual growth that "one day you just wake up, and you're different." This very common myth in Catholic culture is, to put it gently, false. How do we know? Because it is false in absolutely every other area of adult life.

You might as well hope to wake up one morning and find that you became a brain surgeon in your sleep. Yet when it comes to the experience of being transformed by the following of Christ, some Catholics suddenly begin to speak and act as though the process were magical. In the past, I have given a number of carefully documented presentations on the theology of evangelization, most of which were received with varying levels of polite indifference. But when we began to use the phrase "*intentional* disciple," people suddenly snapped to attention. Of course, "*unintentional* discipleship" is impossible, but using explicit language like "intentional discipleship" seemed to break the mysterious spell that makes it difficult for many Catholics to think and speak of discipleship in meaningful, real-life ways.

How then do we become disciples? By acting like Simon Peter:

> Jesus said to Simon, "Do not be afraid; henceforth you will be catching men." And when they had brought their boats to land, they left everything and followed him. (Luke 5:10–11)

Simon's experience was not exceptional, either in human terms or in the tradition of the Church. No one voluntarily sheds his or her job, home, and whole way of life accidently or unconsciously. Simon Peter's "drop the net" decision is what we mean by "intentional." From the moment he dropped his nets to follow Jesus, he was a disciple.

Peter did not, of course, know what the full ramifications of that decision would be for himself or for the world.

No disciple ever does. And it would take the rest of his life to become a saint. But he had consciously begun the journey.

It is the same with us. Intentional discipleship is not accidental or merely cultural. It is not just a matter of "following the rules." A disciple's primary motivation comes from within, out of a Holy Spirit-given "hunger and thirst for righteousness." All things serve and flow from the central thing: the worship and love of the Blessed Trinity with one's whole heart, soul, mind, and strength, and therefore the love of one's neighbor as oneself.

To be sure, following what God has revealed through his Church (journeys two and three) is an essential part of the life of the disciple. In fact, the sacraments and full participation in the life of the Church are central moments in the relationship with Christ. But discipleship begins when "adult persons at last have the occasion to hear the kerygma, renew their own baptism, consciously choose Christ as their own personal Lord and Savior, and commit themselves actively in the life of their Church."[10]

What is the kerygma? Briefly, *kerygma* is the Greek term referring to the preaching or proclamation of the basic outline of the life, passion, death, and resurrection of Jesus Christ. The kerygma is the essential nucleus of the Gospel that awakens initial Christian faith. It leads a person to be able to say, "Jesus is Lord!" Kerygma is what Pope John Paul II described as

---

[10] "Father Cantalamessa on Christ Yesterday and Today (Part II)," Zenit, December 2, 2005 (online at www.zenit.org/article-14735?l=english, as of May 8, 2012).

"the initial ardent proclamation by which a person is one day overwhelmed and brought to the decision to entrust himself to Jesus Christ by faith."[11]

One of the obstacles to calling our own to discipleship is that few Catholics have ever heard of the kerygma or the "Great Story of Jesus" (to borrow a wonderful phrase from Father Robert Barron), and even fewer know what the kerygma contains or have heard it preached clearly. Father Mike and I learned that lesson vividly while giving a presentation on the thresholds to the evangelization committee of a large archdiocese. I casually referred to the kerygma during our presentation. At the question-and-answer time, a brave and honest woman raised her hand and said, "I don't know what the kerygma is." Then she turned to the rest of the committee and continued, "I don't think most of us here know either. Do you know what the kerygma is?" We looked on with a sinking feeling as most of the leaders of evangelization in this archdiocese started vigorously shaking their heads no. That's why I will be devoting the whole of chapter 10 to discussing the kerygma, the nucleus of the Gospel that awakens Christian faith.

EXAMINING OUR PARADIGM

In the twenty-first century, Catholic pastoral practice is still largely based upon what could be called an "infant paradigm," rather than an "adult paradigm." What do I mean? We often function as though the initiation of a young child

---

[11] Pope John Paul II, *Catechesi Tradendae*, 25.

into the faith is the practical spiritual norm. A baby is not capable of personal faith or personal sin and cannot put any obstacles in the way of receiving the graces given in baptism. When an infant is baptized, the faith of the baby's parents, godparents, and the Church substitute for the child's faith. Nothing can be asked of a baby.

This paradigm also assumes that a baptized child will pick up the Catholic faith from the family and the parish as naturally and inevitably as he or she learns language and culture. The faith is communicated, and the child trustingly accepts and believes it. The child will inherit a stable, life-long religious identity and practice from the family and the parish, a Catholic identity that will move seamlessly into adulthood, resulting in slow spiritual growth over a lifetime. There is little expectation of distinct internal turning points, much less of an overt "conversion" experience.

Craig Pohl was born and raised in a community where the infant paradigm still rules. Westphalia, Michigan, is historically 95 percent Catholic, and roughly 80 percent of its Catholic citizens attend Mass regularly. Craig was a sophomore in high school before he realized that not everyone was Catholic. Father James Conlon, pastor of Craig's parish, St. Mary's, told me that the region is sometimes referred to as "the Holy Land" by Michiganders. As Craig observed:

> Catholic culture was so thick, and practice is strong. In small communities, you know, you just do it. Practice is strong but there was little spirit. It is very easy to fall within the boundaries of the rules set for you. You just do the bare minimum — go to Mass

on Sundays and holy days. It was a very common thing to get together on Friday night and just have a good time (sports, sex, alcohol) and go to Mass on Sunday because that is what you do.

Despite a level of Mass attendance that verges on the miraculous by Western standards, Father James and Father Dennis Howard, pastor of neighboring Most Holy Trinity Parish in Fowler, joined together in 2009 to hire Craig Pohl as a full-time evangelist. As Father James put it:

> Why would you bring in an evangelist even though Mass attendance is high? When people ask, I say because we all need to grow in our relationship with Christ. I was witnessing people who were struggling to remain Catholic. They were coming to me to talk about something deep — family issues, children, their own interior struggles. I witnessed that the old certainties had fallen away. Most don't have lives of prayer; they know rote prayers. I kept trying to explain that it is about you in relationship in Christ; it is not an insurance policy.

> We identified adult formation as a need. Knowledge of the faith is at a very, very low level. The challenge is for parishes to offer opportunities for parishioners to grow in their faith, not just as faithful Roman Catholics but as active disciples of Christ in the world.

When we act as though the experience of conversion is rare rather than normative, we are operating out of the infant paradigm. We are operating out of that paradigm whenever we do not explicitly challenge teen and adult Catholics to become intentional disciples. In contrast, an adult paradigm of evangelization must become the new pastoral norm in our postmodern culture. We must be convinced that *all* the baptized — unless they die early or are incapable of making such a decision — will eventually be called to make a personal choice to live as a disciple of Jesus Christ in the midst of his Church. In the words of Pope Benedict XVI:

> Faith is above all a personal, intimate encounter with Jesus, and to experience his closeness, his friendship, his love; only in this way does one learn to know him ever more, and to love and follow him ever more. May this happen to each one of us.[12]

---

[12] Pope Benedict XVI, General Audience, October 21, 2009 (available online at http://www.vatican.va/holy_father/benedict_xvi/audiences/2009/documents/hf_ben-xvi_aud_20091021_en.html, as of May 8, 2012).

CHAPTER 3

The Fruit of Discipleship

We're really at the dawn of Christianity.

CARDINAL JEAN-MARIE LUSTIGER[1]

In October 2011, I spent a few days with the parishioners and staff of Christ the King Parish in Ann Arbor, Michigan. This relatively small parish (nine hundred families) is an absolute standout by anyone's standards. First of all, Christ the King (CTK) has produced a significant number of priestly vocations over its several decades of existence. Nearly thirty priests who have emerged out of Christ the King now serve in four different dioceses and five religious communities. One of those priests was recently consecrated auxiliary bishop for the Archdiocese of Detroit.

An additional twenty young men associated with the parish are in various stages of priestly formation as I write this. Eight of the Diocese of Lansing's current twenty-seven seminarians are from Christ the King; two others come from Most Holy Trinity in Fowler, where Craig Pohl serves as a full-time evangelist. These two small,

---

[1] John L. Allen, Jr., "Big Picture at World Youth Day: 'It's the Evangelicals, Stupid!'" *National Catholic Reporter*, August 19, 2011 (online at http://ncronline.org/blogs/all-things-catholic/big-picture-world-youth-day-it%E2%80%99s-evangelicals-stupid, as of May 8, 2012).

evangelizing parishes have together produced a remarkable 37 percent of their diocese's seminarians. And the next generation is right behind. During my stay at CTK, I met two remarkably poised and articulate high school seniors who were planning on entering college seminary the next year.

The ecclesial vocations emerging at CTK are by no means limited to the priesthood. Eight men have been ordained to the permanent diaconate: four now serve CTK, and the other four serve in neighboring parishes. There are also nine women in various stages of religious formation. The Servants of God's Love, a homegrown community of sisters, were very visible at the parish Mass. The Servants of the Word, an ecumenical but majority Catholic community of brothers with long-standing ties to CTK, has fifty professed men and fifty more in formation.

A REMARKABLE PARISH

Eleven lay faculty members from Sacred Heart Major Seminary in Detroit also attend Christ the King. One of them is Francisco "Paco" Gavrilides, who worked in evangelization and Latin American missions for many years and now teaches homiletics at Sacred Heart. He described the Mass at CTK as "absolutely alive, reverent, and expectant, a shared experience of God."

Before I spoke to Paco, I had already been moved by the atmosphere at the two Masses I attended. It wasn't that the elements of the Mass were different, although they were well and carefully celebrated. It was something else. I could *feel* a spiritual energy that I have hardly ever experienced before at Mass, as though the intensity of the prayer of those gathered lifted my own prayer to a new level. I mentioned this to several parishioners, and they told me that what I had experienced was normal. This difference may be one reason why a recent survey by the parish found that 98 percent of parishioners attend Mass at CTK or elsewhere every Sunday.

A remarkable sense of personal responsibility and service marks the community. Paco observed: "There is a sense that God is at work and can work through any individual in the parish. If there is a need for a particular ministry, people are just willing to do it."

A large chunk of the Catholic service agencies in the area were started and are staffed by CTK parishioners. Hope Clinic offers free medical and dental care to seven thousand patients every year. A local crisis-pregnancy center, an independent Catholic school, a remarkable prison ministry, and Renewal Ministries, which evangelizes in twenty-five countries, also were all founded by parishioners. The head of Renewal Ministries, Ralph Martin, is also director of the only pontifical degree program in the New Evangelization in the world (at Sacred Heart Major Seminary). In December 2011, Ralph was appointed by Pope Benedict XVI to a five-year term as a consultor to the Pontifical Council for the New Evangelization.

As Paco put it, "Because of the heart to love and serve the Lord, the financial generosity of the parish is unbelievable." One story, which I heard from three different sources, has clearly become part of CTK's identity. Father Ed Fride has pastored CTK for nineteen years, and this is his version:

We had a Ugandan bishop visiting us. His cathedral had been destroyed, and he had to borrow $65,000 to rebuild. Problems with the loan left him in legal trouble, and he was on the verge of losing his cathedral altogether. I told him to mention his need in his homily, and then at announcement time, we'd take up a second collection to support him. We had a couple hundred thousand in our rainy-day fund, and after the second collection, I asked the congregation if they would agree to take any additional funds needed to make up the $65,000 from this fund. The show of hands in favor was unanimous. We ended up receiving so much money in the second collection that we only had to take $20,000 or $30,000 out of the rainy-day fund to cover the total. The bishop went home with $65,000 and rebuilt his cathedral, and our rainy-day fund was completely replenished in a couple of weeks.

Father Ed said that this kind of generosity is common at CTK. "We make a point of making sure that 10 percent of our gross income is going outside the parish, so we tithe to the external Church."

Several parishioners tried to lower my expectations. "We're not perfect; we have our problems too," they assured me. All of which I know is true. But in one sense it doesn't matter. Christ the King isn't perfect, but it is *real*. After working in three hundred parishes, I have a fairly acute sense of "parochial normal." I know lots of amazing Catholics in very active parishes. But I've never seen or heard of a whole parish community functioning at the level of CTK.

I've never been in a Catholic parish where the lived spiritual norm was mature discipleship and apostleship.

DISCIPLESHIP IS CENTRAL

As Paco said, "Discipleship is absolutely central to the parish." The parish mission statement reads, in part, "Surrendered to the Lord Jesus in the power of the Spirit in the heart of the Church." Father Ed put it this way in a 2007 interview with the *National Catholic Register*:

> The spirituality of the parish, in which a personal relationship with Jesus is continually stressed, is key.... We began as, and still are, part of the charismatic renewal, again where a living, active relationship with Jesus is encouraged.[2]

This is what he said to me:

> As pastor, you are the primary evangelist of your people. If you don't know Jesus in a personal way, how can you introduce him to your people? There is an ongoing, constant theme in my homilies: that people need to surrender their lives to Jesus. If you haven't given your life to Jesus, here's how and here's what it looks like in a Catholic context. The core thing is that it always has to come back to the Eucharist.

---

[2] Bob Horning, "1 Parish, 15 Seminarians," *National Catholic Register*, June 26, 2007.

Invite people to live with him and for him, anchor people in the Eucharist, and they won't wander off.

The parish has had perpetual Eucharistic Adoration for the past ten years. Father Ed felt strongly that Eucharistic Adoration was an important factor in the large number of priestly vocations: "Perpetual adoration in a parish significantly raises the prominence and visibility of the Eucharistic Lord."

One of the things I immediately noticed at Sunday Mass was that no single age group or gender predominated. There were teens and young adults mixing seamlessly with middle-aged and older adults. And there were lots of children. Father Ed joked, "This parish is a cry room with a tabernacle attached." He made it clear that making disciples of the children is a major priority:

> There is a lot of intentionality in our approach to evangelizing our kids. We have a really, really good K–12 program.... We want our children to know God, that he is real, he wants to be their friend. By the time they receive First Communion, they are literally vibrating at the touch of the Holy Spirit; they are so excited that they can hardly stand still.

> We also have the best confirmation program. We [with other local Christian groups] have a middle school camp for boys and girls, where we help kids have a huge experience of God, and we encourage all who are preparing for confirmation to attend. And we have a great high school youth program. The Kairos retreat [at the regional Catholic high

school] is having a huge impact on high school seniors.

Put that sort of intentionality together with a parish culture where adult discipleship is routinely modeled and normative, where there is a high number of intact families, with both fathers and mothers eager to pass on the faith to their children, and suddenly what is happening at CTK begins to seem inevitable.

A parish like Christ the King highlights what is at stake in our present failure to foster the discipleship of all the baptized. Many things lie in the balance, but certainly these four:

1. The eternal happiness in God — the salvation — of every human being.
2. The complete fruition of the Mass and the sacraments.
3. The next generation of Catholic leaders, saints, and apostles: priestly, religious, and secular.
4. The fulfillment of the Church's mission on earth.

The good news is that I have seen the same remarkable fruitfulness begin to emerge in every parish that calls its own to intentional discipleship in an effective and sustained way.

The Experience of Sacred Heart Parish

We met Carol McGee and Sacred Heart Parish in Boise, Idaho, fourteen years ago, when she and two other lay leaders drove over the mountains in a snowstorm to attend their first Called & Gifted workshop. Carol headed up her parish's faith formation and evangelization efforts. A few years previously the parish had started offering Evangelization Retreats for adults centered on the renewal of the sacraments of initiation. The power of the Holy Spirit unleashed through that retreat experience had generated a new demand for discernment. So they came to us.

Today I cannot begin to count the number of Sacred Heart parishioners who have told me that their lives were dramatically changed by going through their Evangelization Retreat. (I find it fascinating that about a quarter of attendees at any given retreat are non-Catholic. In Boise, Baptists come to Catholics to be evangelized!) Carol estimates that about 25 percent of adults at Sacred Heart are now intentional disciples. Many of these people had been away from the Church for years and are now on fire with the desire to follow Christ. And their passion has changed the life of the community.

Both Mass attendance and giving have gone up, resulting in the highest per-capita giving in the diocese. Forty percent of parishioners are involved in ministries, and 75 to 80 percent of those have gone through Evangelization Retreats. Parishioners were deeply involved in crafting the parish motto: "Being a Beacon of Christ's Love." The parish is dedicated to making a huge impact on the Church and the world around them. The question they posed to themselves in discerning their mission was: "Would anyone besides parishioners notice if the parish wasn't here? We want the answer to be a resounding Yes!"

In pursuit of that goal, new and often nontraditional ministries have formed. A healing prayer team formed, made up of people who had discerned charisms of intercessory prayer and healing. After being trained in healing prayer, they now pray for parishioners at Sacred Heart and other parishes. Carol says that incredible healings have occurred — physical, emotional, and spiritual.

Other new ministries include In-Touch Ministry (telephoning parishioners just to "keep in touch"), English for Immigrants, No-One Dies Alone, Celebrate Recovery, and Dominican Overseas Education & Relief Service in Central America. A team brings the Evangelization Retreat to parishes in Idaho and other states. They also have a Called & Gifted teaching team that travels throughout Idaho.

In addition, the parish has discerned a communal charism of mercy, which has expressed itself in both spiritual and corporal works of mercy, such as prayer at a neighborhood abortion clinic (now closed) and an area dinner for the poor. The parish was heavily involved in opening two Catholic Worker houses focused on contemplation and action. Parishioners participated in a citywide effort to support a day shelter for the homeless, worked with Habitat for Humanity, and cooperated with Catholic Charities to help refugees and immigrants by collecting household goods, teaching English lessons, and sponsoring a Mass in Swahili.

One woman's experience in particular has changed the lives of many. Ellen Piper is a licensed social worker who leads Boise's Catholic Worker community. Ellen helped found the first day shelter for the homeless in the state and recruited and equipped an entire homeless men's firefighting team. She also started two transitional houses for homeless men and women while getting her M.A. in social work. It's all a long way from where Ellen began twelve years ago as a quietly restless parishioner. This is Ellen's description of how her journey began:

> I had a nagging sense of a call to do something. I was praying and saying, "Lord, what do you want me to do?" I had a dream in which I heard the words, "Do the works of mercy." I asked a priest what the "works of mercy" were. Then I went on the Evangelization Retreat, and something set me on fire. I decided to go work with our St. Vincent de Paul Society. It seemed safe. Then I went to the Called & Gifted workshop. I scored high on mercy on the gifts inventory and thought, "This is supposed to be what you are doing."
>
> Without the Called & Gifted workshop this wouldn't have happened. Seeing the gift of mercy on that inventory answer sheet really empowered me. I thought that if I was empowered by God, then I had some courage to go and step out of the parish. If the Called & Gifted and that Evangelization Retreat hadn't come into the parish, you wouldn't be talking to me right now. I wouldn't have stepped out.

CULTIVATING DISCIPLESHIP

We have seen it happen over and over. *The presence of a significant number of disciples changes everything*: a parish's spiritual tone, energy level, attendance, bottom line, and what parishioners ask of their leaders. Disciples pray with passion. Disciples worship. Disciples love the Church and serve her with energy and joy. Disciples give lavishly. Disciples hunger to learn more about their faith. Disciples fill every formation class in a parish or diocese. Disciples manifest charisms and discern vocations. They clamor to discern God's call because they long to live it. Disciples evangelize because they have really good news to share. Disciples share their faith with their children. Disciples care about the poor and about issues of justice. Disciples take risks for the Kingdom of God.

The Holy Spirit is planting charisms and vocations of amazing diversity in the hearts of all his people. Like the graces of the sacraments, they are real, but they are not magic. Just as the gifts of children must be fostered deliberately and with great energy by parents if their children are to reach their full potential, so vocations must be fostered by the Church.

In this area, we are not asking for too much; we are settling for too little. God is not asking us to call forth the gifts and vocations of a few people; he is asking us to call forth the gifts and vocations of millions. Our problem is not that there is a shortage of vocations but that we do not have the support systems and leadership in place to foster the vast majority of the vocations that God has given us. *Most fundamentally, when we fail to call our own to discipleship, we are unwittingly pushing away the vast majority of the vocations God has given us.*

Although we hardly ever talk about it, the whole Church bears responsibility for the charisms and personal vocations of each member:

... The Church fulfills her mission when she guides every member of the faithful to discover and live his or her own vocation in freedom and to bring it to fulfillment in charity.

... Indeed, God with his call reaches the call of each individual, and the Spirit, who abides deep within each disciple (cf. 1 Jn 3:24), gives himself to each Christian with different charisms and special signs. Each one, therefore, must be helped to embrace the gift entrusted to him as a completely unique person, and to hear the words which the Spirit of God personally addresses to him.[3]

One moment stands out from the days when I was just beginning to know Father Michael Sweeney, who was then my pastor in Seattle. The Catherine of Siena Institute was not even dreamed of. A group of young Catholic friends was spending an evening with Father Michael. Some of us were recent converts, some lifelong Catholics. We were all eager to live as disciples and apostles.

I can't remember what triggered it, but suddenly Father Michael turned to us and said something I have never forgotten: *"You are the evidence that my priesthood is bearing fruit."*

I remember that my first response was surprise. I thought: "Father Michael is talking like he's a *human be-*

---

[3]   Pope John Paul II, *Pastores Dabo Vobis* (On the Formation of Priests), 40 (online at www.vatican.va/holy_father/john_paul_ii/apost_exhortations/ documents/hf_jp-ii_exh_25031992_pastores-dabo-vobis_en.html, as of May 8, 2012).

ing. [I was still a little unclear in those days about how completely human priests are.] As though he is like us, as though he doesn't already know for sure. He is looking for signs that his vocation, his life, is making a difference. Who knew that priests are asking the same questions that we are asking?" What I didn't know then was that Father Michael was speaking of the priestly task of governance. Governance is one of the three *munera*, or tasks, of the ministerial priesthood: teaching, sanctifying, and governing.

PASTORAL GOVERNANCE

The Church puts it this way:

> … The ministerial priesthood is at the service of the common priesthood. It is directed at the unfolding of the baptismal grace of all Christians. (CCC 1547)

> The ministerial priesthood differs in essence from the common priesthood of the faithful because it confers a sacred power for the service of the faithful. (CCC 1592)

St. Paul conceived of leadership in the Church as ordered toward fostering the spiritual growth and mission of *all* the baptized:

> And his gifts were that some should be apostles, some prophets, some evangelists, some pastors and teachers, to equip the saints for the work of ministry, for building up the body of Christ, until we all

attain to the unity of the faith and of the knowledge of the Son of God, to mature manhood, to
the measure of the stature of the fulness of Christ.
(Ephesians 4:11–13)

Church teaching spells out in considerable detail what
this would mean. Priests are to do the following:

- *Cooperate* with laity in their mission to the world.
- *Listen* to laity.
- *Recognize* lay expertise.
- *Awaken and deepen* lay co-responsibility.
- Confidently *entrust* duties to laity.
- *Invite* lay *initiative.*
- *Help* all *explore and discern vocation.*
- *Form and support* secular apostles.[4]

The task of governance also requires that priests recognize, uncover with faith, acknowledge with joy, foster with
diligence, appreciate, judge, discern, coordinate, put to good
use, and have "heartfelt esteem" for the charisms of all the
baptized.[5]

---

[4] See *Presbyterorum Ordinis* (Decree on the Life and Ministry of Priests),
    9. Available online at www.vatican.va/archive/hist_councils/ii_vatican_
    council/documents/vat-ii_decree_19651207_presbyterorum-ordinis_
    en.html, as of May 8, 2012. Also see Pope John Paul II, *Pastores Dabo
    Vobis*, 59; 74.

[5] *Lumen Gentium* (Dogmatic Constitution on the Church), 30 (online at
    www.vatican.va/archive/hist_councils/ii_vatican_council/documents/
    vat-ii_const_19641121_lumen-gentium_en.html), as of May 8, 2012;
    Presbyterorum Ordinis, 9; Pope John Paul II, *Pastores Dabo Vobis*, 40, 74;
    Pope John Paul II, *Christifideles Laici*, 32.

The spiritual forces unleashed in the Christian community through conversion and ongoing discipleship will evoke and, in a real sense, demand governance. Lived fatherhood with real children — especially adult children — is a true relationship. As spiritual fathers, priests call forth and foster the baptismal priesthood. The needs, gifts, and initiatives of lay disciples draw out the fullness of teaching, sanctifying, and governing from the ordained.

Father Mike Fones knows how rewarding the experience of governance can be:

> Of the three aspects of priesthood, I would say I am most powerfully drawn to the royal aspect. I feel my priesthood is coming to its fullest fruition when people discern their call from God and begin to live it in the world. My experience tells me that this aspect of pastoral governance — the expression of the priest's royal office shared with Christ — is incredibly neglected. I often wonder what it would look like if a pastor intentionally focused on this aspect of his priesthood; how would parishioners respond if they were challenged to consciously discern their gifts and call (and given help to do so), and then intentionally supported by the parish in living that call?
>
> I also wonder if a whole set of young men aren't being drawn to the priesthood because their call is most closely associated with the royal aspect of a priest's office. I know priests whose priesthood is most deeply felt when they're celebrating the sacraments, and others for whom teaching and preach-

ing are the cornerstone of their lives. Might there not be men who would respond to an invitation from Christ to be a priest if they saw the royal function expressed more clearly and powerfully?

Gaurav Shroff is one of those young men. Gaurav began life as a Hindu in a highly educated Indian family. He first encountered Christianity through the beauty of Gregorian chant. Today he is a diocesan seminarian for the Archdiocese of Atlanta; if all goes well, he will be ordained in 2013. Gaurav has a similar vision for his own priestly ministry:

> Evangelization and the vocation of the laity will be the central passion of my ministry as a diocesan priest. I see my future role as someone who leads, sanctifies, and teaches the laity, not as passive recipients. I shall be someone who calls out their gifts, talents, charisms, so that the Christ's lay faithful can be equipped to bring the Gospel to the world, and share in the Church's mission.[6]

PARTICIPATION OF THE LAITY

A dramatic increase in the number of baptized Catholics in the nineteenth and twentieth centuries is putting tremendous pressure on the priest-lay person relationship. The global Catholic population has *quadrupled* in the last century

---

[6] Nirmala Carvalho, "Gregorian music led me to Christ, says Gaurav," Asia News.it, April 13, 2010 (online at www.asianews.it/news-en/ Gregorian-music-led-me-to-Christ,-says-Gaurav-18127.html, as of May 8, 2012).

(from 291.4 million in 1910 to 1,196 million as of 2010).[7] Thirty-four million additional Catholics joined us between January 1, 2008, and December 31, 2009. The primary "culprit" behind the global priest shortage is success beyond the wildest dreams of our great-grandparents. Vastly improved health care and access to better food and clean water resulted in a huge drop in childhood mortality in the twentieth century. Meanwhile, the faith has spread like wildfire in large areas of the previously non-Christian global South. These are the kinds of problems that we want to have, but as with all changes, they brought with them unintended effects.

Priests have always loomed larger in the Catholic imagination than in actual fact. There were 48,415 *more* priests in the world in 2010 than in 1950 and 57,652 *more* seminarians than in 1950.[8] But because of staggering growth in the number of Catholics, bishops and priests make up only a tiny fraction (0.035 percent) of the body Catholic. As of 2010, 417,340 priests and bishops were serving approximately 1,195,582,000 men and women.[9] It is the laity — the common priesthood — that constitutes 99.962 percent of the Church (excluding deacons, who are ordained). In 1978, lay Catholics were only 10.8 percent of the Church's recognized workforce.[10] Thirty

[7]   Johnson and Ross, *Atlas of Global Christianity: 1910–2010*, p. 95; "Presentation of Pontifical Yearbook 2012," Vatican Information Service, March 12, 2012.

[8]   Bryan T. Froehle and Mary L. Gautier, *Global Catholicism: Portrait of a World Church* (Maryknoll, NY: Orbis Books, 2003), pp. 31 and 35.

[9]   "Presentation of Pontifical Yearbook 2012."

[10] John Thavis, "Church's International Contours Changed Under Pope John Paul II," Catholic News Service (online at www.catholicnews.com/ jpii/stories/story19.htm, as of May 8, 2012).

years later, in 2009, lay catechists and missionaries (excluding religious and seminarians) made up roughly 72 percent of the 4.8-million-person "Workforce for the Church's Apostolate."[11]

This is, I think, an example of what Pope Benedict XVI has called a *novità di Dio*, an "innovation of God." The Holy Father quoted a maxim of St. Bonaventure: *Opera Christi non deficiunt, sed proficiunt* — "Christ's works do not go backward but forward."[12] In the twenty-first century, God seems to be doing something new again to meet the needs of our time. Millions of lay men and women are answering God's call to evangelize, form, and nurture the millions of new brothers and sisters God is sending us every year.

Priests and deacons participate by right in the pastoral office of Christ as coworkers of the bishop. But all formally recognized parish and diocesan lay leaders — formal or informal, paid or volunteer — participate in the pastoral office *by delegation* from their bishop or pastor. (We are used to this in the ministry of teaching. At a practical level, most of the catechetical work of the Church has been carried out by the non-ordained for centuries.) Therefore, all pastoral leaders participate in governance at different levels. *All* of us need to be able to say to emerging disciples around us, "You are the evidence that my ministry is bearing fruit."

---

[11] "Vatican — World Mission Day: Catholic Church Statistics," Fides, October 21, 2011 (online at www.fides.org/aree/news/newsdet.php?idnews=30147&lan=eng, as of May 8, 2012).

[12] Pope Benedict XVI, General Audience, March 10, 2010 (online at http://www.vatican.va/holy_father/benedict_xvi/audiences/2010/documents/hf_ben-xvi_aud_20100310_en.html, as of May 8, 2012).

No matter how many institutions we sustain or how much activity goes on in our parish or diocese, if new intentional disciples are not regularly emerging in our midst, our ministry is not bearing its most essential fruit. Just as parental gifts don't get exercised if you have no children, so the expression of the pastoral office is greatly attenuated and, in a real sense, suppressed by the lack of lay disciples and apostles to ask for and to receive it.

THE HEART OF VOCATION

"He brought him to Jesus" [Jn 1:42]. In a way, *this is the heart of all the Church's pastoral work on behalf of vocations*, in which she cares for the birth and growth of vocations, making use of the gifts and responsibilities, of the charisms and ministry she has received from Christ and his Spirit.[13]

In the Catholic tradition, the word *vocation* is not a synonym for *ecclesial career*. A vocation is a supernatural mystery that emerges from a sustained encounter with Christ. It is a transforming, sanctifying path and work of love to which Christ calls us. A vocation builds on our natural qualities but carries us far beyond what we would imagine. The classic example of this principle is Simon Peter. As theologian Hans Urs von Balthasar observed, "Simon, the fisherman, before his meeting with Christ, how-

---

[13] Pope John Paul II, *Pastores Dabo Vobis*, 38, emphasis added.

ever thoroughly he might have searched within himself, could not possibly have found a trace of Peter."[14]

Discipleship is the necessary seedbed without which Christian vocations of any kind cannot germinate and grow. Vocational discernment must be rooted in a rich and deep conversation among fellow disciples. After Father Gregory Jensen (an Orthodox priest and psychologist) and I had a long conversation about the state of discipleship in our respective communions, he wrote this blog post:

> I would argue that what typically happens is that we ask people who haven't yet repented (and so who are not yet disciples of Christ) to take on work meant for apostles. Not only do we entrust philanthropic work to those who are not yet disciples of Christ, we also ask them to undertake evangelism and catechesis and serve on parish council. We might also bless them to attend seminary and ordain them to the diaconate or priesthood.
>
> We do this because we are ourselves in the main not disciples of Jesus Christ. Having neglected repentance in my life, I am indifferent to it in yours.... Because we neglect repentance and the spiritual formation of the laity as disciples, we essentially ask people to carry burdens that are beyond their strength. Without an awareness of the gifts Christ has given them personally in baptism and without the proper spiritual formation in the exercise of

---

[14] Hans Urs von Balthasar, *Prayer* (San Francisco: Ignatius, 1986), p. 49.

those gifts — and this includes an ethical formation in the limits that these gifts impose on my will
— is it any wonder that people fail? We cannot ask
even good and talented people who are not yet disciples to undertake the works appropriate only to
apostles. And yet we do this all the time.[15]

Discerning ecclesial vocations, especially priestly vocations, is critical for the American Church, because half of
our currently active diocesan priests will retire by 2018.[16]
Our Catholic population is about 77.7 million, approximately 75 percent higher than it was forty years ago, when
it was served by roughly the same number of parishes.[17]
Most dioceses in the country are feeling a shortage of clergy. The good news is that if we evangelize, it is not hard to
turn our parishes into rich seedbeds of fertile vocational
soil. I saw this happen at Blessed Sacrament in Seattle, a
Dominican parish with lots of young-adult disciples.

When he was still pastor there, Father Michael Sweeney started a parish discernment group that was open to all
single men and women who thought they might be called
to an ecclesial vocation. It was a confidential group that

---

[15] Father Gregory Jensen, "Repentance and Discipleship," Koinonia blog,
April 15, 2011 (online at http://palamas.info/?p=6060, as of May 8,
2012).

[16] Mark Gray, "Facing a Future with Fewer Catholic Priests," *Our Sunday
Visitor,* June 27, 2010.

[17] Jerry Filteau, "Study finds US Catholic parishes growing larger, more
complex," *National Catholic Reporter,* August 2, 2011 (online at http://
ncronline.org/news/study-finds-us-catholic-parishes-growing-larger-
more-complex, as of May 8, 2012).

provided a safe space in which to do an initial exploration of the possibility of priestly or religious vocation free
of pressure from family and friends. All members went
through the Called & Gifted process in order to become
more aware of the presence of charisms in their lives and
of the communal charisms of the communities they were
investigating. They met once a month to discuss Church
teachings on vocation, religious life, and priesthood or to
talk about a visit they had made to a religious community
or vocations director. It was a simple process but remarkably fruitful. As a result, eight parishioners over two years
entered Benedictine, Dominican, and Trappist communities as well as the diocesan priesthood.

DISCERNING CHARISMS

Our parishes need to become places where it is normal for
adult Catholics to ask, "What is God calling me to?" Over
the years we have discovered that a powerful way to foster
a parish culture of discernment is by beginning with the
discernment of personal charisms.

Charisms are some of the many graces that we receive
in baptism and confirmation. A charism is "a favor" or (in St.
Thomas Aquinas's terminology) a "gratuitous grace" given
to a member of the body of Christ to empower him or her
to build up the Church and to witness Christ to the world.
Charisms are supernaturally empowered ways in which
God's mercy, love, healing, truth, beauty, and provision will
reach others through us. Most importantly, charisms, unlike
natural talents or skills, can never be kept to ourselves or
used deliberately for evil.

St. Paul and many of the early Church Fathers, and later St. Thomas Aquinas, wrote in considerable detail about the existence and significance of charisms in the Church's life and mission.[18] The first discussion of charisms to take place at an ecumenical council occurred in the midst of a discussion of the apostolic mission of the laity at the Second Vatican Council. This is one reason the *Decree on the Apostolate of the Laity* states:

> Indeed, everyone should diligently prepare himself for the apostolate, this preparation being the more urgent in adulthood. For the advance of age brings with it a more open mind, enabling each person to detect more readily the talents with which God has enriched his soul and to exercise more effectively those charisms which the Holy Spirit has bestowed on him for the good of his brethren.[19]

In the course of the Called & Gifted process, we deal with twenty-four of the most common charisms. Charisms like evangelism and encouragement can powerfully move others to open their lives to Christ. Charisms of teaching and wisdom can help remove impediments to freely choosing personal faith and discipleship. Gifts of healing, intercessory prayer, and hospitality can enable the recipient to

[18] Sherry Anne Weddell, *The Catholic Spiritual Gifts Resource Guide* (Colorado Springs, CO: Siena Institute Press, 2003), pp. 4-6.

[19] *Apostolicam Actuositatem* (Decree on the Apostolate of the Laity), 30 (available online at www.vatican.va/archive/hist_councils/ii_vatican_council/documents/vat-ii_decree_19651118_apostolicam-actuositatem_en.html, as of May 8, 2012).

cooperate in Christ's redemptive work by healing others. And charisms of leadership, administration, mercy, and giving enable the recipient to cooperate in Christ's redemptive work by healing society.

Like personal vocations, charisms almost always manifest *after* the point in our life when our faith becomes personal and we begin the journey of discipleship. They may also manifest for the first time *when* we meet a person or situation for which that particular gift is needed. In short, charisms tend to show up at the mysterious intersection where the Church and the world cry out to God in need and a disciple takes up his or her call to follow Jesus. When the Catholic community begins to foster discernment of the charisms, the disciple begins to experience the living reality that "I have been anointed and sent by Christ." Indeed, the discernment of one's charisms becomes a vital clue to one's "general area of call" — the arena of life for which God has equipped the person. And this, in turn, facilitates discernment of other calls.

Catholics who discern charisms often do so as a way to begin discerning personal vocation. We have had a number of men and women use the Called & Gifted process as a first step in discerning a call to priesthood or religious life. One fascinating corollary of all this is that a charism carries with it *a certain leadership (formal or informal)* in the particular area of giftedness. We've seen over and over, with the 65,000 Catholics who have experienced the Called & Gifted process, that recognizing one's charisms unleashes amazing creativity and initiative.

Scott Moyer, a high-tech entrepreneur, said that he knew that "he wasn't called to be a priest, and yet it was as though there was a part of him that was never going to be able to live." Discerning his charisms named his restlessness and propelled Scott into full-time work as a parish director of adult faith formation and head of our Called & Gifted team in the San Francisco Bay area. Another man, a retired military officer in Virginia, discerned a charism of administration and offered to serve his pastor for two years as an unpaid full-time administrator!

Genuine discernment can also move people in the opposite direction. In Atlanta, three Called & Gifted alumni told me that they had recognized a call to leave full-time ministry and return to the marketplace as secular apostles, something they would not have considered legitimate before. One young man in Seattle, who later became a fully professed Dominican, summed up his experience of discernment this way: "It was a real choice. You made being a lay apostle sound so interesting."

If we do not see the parish as a center of evangelization and apostolic formation, we are denying priests and their pastoral collaborators one of the great, abiding joys of ministry and one of the most powerful protections against cynicism and burnout. It is incredibly satisfying and a profound fulfillment of the pastoral office to see people come alive spiritually and personally. It recharges our faith to watch the Holy Spirit transform lives and to hear stories of God using "ordinary" Catholics in extraordinary ways; to witness twenty-first-century Mother Teresas and Dorothy Days, Dominics, and Frederick Ozanams emerging in our midst. As Father Mike Fones told me after his first year with us, "This experience has transformed my whole understanding of priesthood and my personal spiritual life as well."

If we focus on making disciples and equipping apostles first, the rest will follow. We won't have to worry about our institutional gaps. The disciples and apostles we form today will found and sustain our institutions and structures tomorrow, and the Holy Spirit will gift and inspire them to do things that we have never dreamed of. What we are called to do is to truly see and then make disciples of the anointed ones who are wandering in and out of our parishes right now.

CHAPTER 4

Grace and the Great Quest

Grace is grace, not magic.

MARK SHEA

In Léon Bloy's novel *The Woman Who Was Poor*, the heroine famously declares, "There is only one sadness, it is to not be a saint."[1] The tragedy of not being a saint is both global and personal, temporal and eternal. A saint's life sends out ripples of grace that bless many within the Church and outside of it. When the fruit of a saint's life is missing, all of us are impoverished, because the impact of the presence or absence of the power of the Holy Spirit doesn't stop at the borders of an individual's earthly life.

But I have to disagree with Bloy. I think that there is a greater sadness than even the lack of individual saints: the *absence of the communal fruit* that God intends to manifest within our Christian communities and networks of saints-in-the-making. This absence is an almost unfathomable loss because it affects the whole human race. We can be deprived of the rivers of prayer, generosity, wisdom, love, creativity, charisms, vocations, and grace that God intends to bless, heal, evangelize, and transform the lives of billions.

---

[1] Léon Bloy, *The Woman Who Was Poor* (London: Sheed & Ward, 1947), p. 354.

Grace is a word that bears the weight of multiple meanings, both in English and in Greek (*charis*). It is at once the *fruit* of God's acting upon us and a free supernatural *gift* of God to help us attain eternal life. Grace empowers our intellects and wills to understand God's will and obey it, yet at the same time it leaves us free to resist if we choose. It is, in a word, love received and given.[2] And what God desires to give through the sacramental graces received by a single man or woman fuels the whole Church's increase in charity and mission (CCC 1134). "The fruit of *all* the sacraments belongs to *all* the faithful," linking them with one another and "binding them to Jesus Christ" (CCC 950, emphasis added).

St. Thomas Aquinas taught that grace heals the soul by helping us recognize the good while empowering us to desire the good, do the good, persevere in the good, and reach glory.[3] Sanctifying grace — the saving grace that makes us participants in the life of the Blessed Trinity and members of the body of Christ — is normally received by older children and adults through a *properly disposed* reception of the sacraments (CCC 1131). What does "properly disposed" mean? Thereby hangs a tale of immense importance.

GRACE AND DISPOSITION

In recent decades, there has been little or no serious discussion at the parish level about how an individual *receiving* the sacraments can prepare his or her heart, soul, and life to do so

---

[2] Pope Benedict XVI, *Caritas in Veritate* ("Charity in Truth"), 5 (online at www.vatican.va/holy_father/benedict_xvi/encyclicals/documents/hf_ben-xvi_enc_20090629_caritas-in-veritate_en.html, as of May 8, 2012).

[3] St. Thomas Aquinas, *Summa Theologiae* II, I, 111, a.3.

fruitfully. Nor do we dream about the amazing things God would do in our midst if the lives of our people were characterized by great spiritual fruitfulness. A Church that understands itself as possessing the "fullness of the means of grace" must yearn for the *fullness of the manifestation* of that grace.

The world waits, longs, for this full manifestation. Yet in many, if not most of our parishes, we have accepted a passive, notional "faith," a general absence of fruit, and a lack of overt manifestation of grace as normal. This distorted sense of what is "normal" has profoundly shaped our parochial culture and pastoral practice, with devastating results.

If our pastoral practice is to be life changing, then we must be acutely aware that the *reception of a valid sacrament* and the *fruitful reception of sacramental grace* are two different but related issues. *Validity* means that the sacrament was truly bestowed and the intended grace made truly present to the person receiving the sacrament. But validity does *not* guarantee that the grace made available *has been actively received and is bearing fruit in that person's life.* What do I mean by this?

The Church has long distinguished between "objective" redemption and "subjective" redemption. By his life, death, and resurrection, Jesus has already reconciled our race with the Father; this is objective redemption. Subjective redemption is the *application* of the saving gifts of Christ to individuals, the *realization* of salvific transformation in each of our lives. Human beings (with the unique exception of the Virgin Mary[4]) contribute nothing whatsoever to the work

---

[4] The ongoing theological debate about the exact nature of Mary's participation in objective and subjective redemption falls outside the scope of this book.

of Christ in objective redemption, but the exercise of our free cooperation with God's grace is central in the drama of subjective redemption.

As adults we can do something infants can't: we can throw up roadblocks or obstacles (*obex*) that stop the grace of God either in whole or in part. Adults and children past the age of reason are not merely passive subjects to whom salvation "happens," as though we were patients anesthetized on a gurney. Rather, we are active agents who are, in the words of Jesus, called to love God with all our heart, soul, mind, and strength (see Mark 12:30). As Augustine famously observed, "God created us without us: but he did not will to save us without us."[5]

The Church uses remarkably strong language in this regard, calling it *superstition* to treat the sacraments as though they were magic and change us without our active cooperation:

> To attribute the efficacy of prayers or of sacramental signs to their mere external performance, *apart from the interior dispositions that they demand*, is to fall into superstition. (CCC 2111, emphasis added)

The Church has traditionally recognized three aspects of the sacraments of baptism, confirmation, and holy orders that bestow a "character" and so can't be repeated. The first aspect is the outward sign — the washing with water in the case of baptism. The second is the permanent "character," or "mark," that the valid sacrament places upon the soul. The

---

[5]   St. Augustine, *Sermo* 169,11,13:PL 38, 923.

third aspect is the actual sacramental grace that is made present. This grace is sometimes referred to as "reality only." Inward justification, "the application of the redemption to the individual,"[6] is the *reality* of baptism. For an adult to be baptized fruitfully, he or she must embrace *both* baptism *and* the baptismal effect, *both* the sacramental sign *and* the inward reality.

This "both/and" embrace is what the Church means by "positive disposition" in the context of the sacraments. It is an eager seeking after God with the hope and expectation that God will show up. "Positive disposition" means we are prepared to change and we actively seek the grace of God in order to do so. It is called *positive* because it includes the expectation that God intends to reveal himself to us, will guide us in the way we should go, and will give us the helps necessary (both internal and external) to enable us to do what he calls us to do.

INTENTION MATTERS

Passively receiving a sacrament is not enough. The grace we receive is directly related to the personal faith, spiritual expectancy, and hunger with which we approach the sacrament. St. Thomas describes how adults who have been validly baptized can receive very different effects of grace — or even none at all:

> Therefore, since all children are equally disposed to Baptism, because they are baptized not in their own

---

6 Aquinas, *Summa Theologiae*, III, q66, a1.

faith, but in that of the Church, they all receive an equal effect in Baptism. Whereas adults, who approach Baptism in their own faith, are not equally disposed to Baptism; for some approach thereto with greater, some with less, devotion. And therefore some receive a greater, some a smaller, share of the grace of newness; just as from the same fire, he receives more heat who approaches nearest to it, although the fire, as far as it is concerned, sends forth its heat equally to all.[7]

The *Catholic Encyclopedia* speaks of the same possibility:

The character imparted by these sacraments is something distinct from the grace imparted by them.... [I]t may even happen, in the reception of these sacraments, that the character is imparted and the grace withheld; the lack of proper dispositions which is sufficient to prevent the reception of the grace may not prevent the reception of the character.

Thus, an adult who receives Baptism without right faith and repentance but with a real intention of receiving the sacrament, obtains the character without the grace.[8]

Whenever I have spoken of this possibility in public, any clergy present — even those passionate about evange-

---

[7]   Ibid., III, q69, a8.

[8]   "Character" in the 1917 *Catholic Encyclopedia* (online at www.newadvent .org/cathen/03586a.htm, as of May 8, 2012).

lization — seemed stunned and bewildered. I have yet to meet a priest or deacon who has told me that this possibility was made explicit during his formation. No wonder we so seldom discuss the possibility that the graces objectively received may not manifest in the lives of individuals and in the midst of our communities. Personal faith plays a significant role for adults even when it comes to a sacrament's *validity*. Not only must an older child or adult intend to receive the sacrament in question, but he or she must also possess a *minimal level of Christian faith* to even validly receive a sacrament:

> Today, the faith-situation of baptized persons is anything but clear, and the Church and its theologians acknowledge two kinds of baptized: believers and nonbelievers. The two are distinguished theologically on the basis of the presence or absence of active personal faith.[9]

What is not yet clear is the minimum amount of faith required of the recipient before the sacrament is validly conferred. As then-Cardinal Ratzinger wrote in 1999:

> Faith belongs to the essence of sacrament. It remains to clarify the juridical question: what level of non-faith would mean that a sacrament has not been effected?[10]

---

[9] Michael G. Lawler, *Marriage and the Catholic Church: Disputed Questions* (Collegeville, MN: Liturgical Press, 2002), p. 51.

[10] Joseph Cardinal Ratzinger, "A propos de la pastorale des divorces remariés," *La Documentation Catholique*, April 4, 1999, 325.

Nor is this the only time Pope Benedict XVI has reflected on this matter:

> During the meeting with clergy in the Diocese of Aosta, which took place 25 July 2005, Pope Benedict XVI spoke of this difficult question: ... "When I was Prefect of the Congregation for the Doctrine of the Faith, I invited various Bishops' Conferences and experts to study this problem: a sacrament celebrated without faith. Whether, in fact, a moment of invalidity could be discovered here because the Sacrament was found to be lacking a fundamental dimension, I do not dare to say. I personally thought so, but from the discussions we had I realized that it is a highly complex problem and ought to be studied further."[11]

In any case, simply going through the motions to please others is not enough for fruitful reception. St. Thomas defines the obstacle of "insincerity" this way:

> A man is said to be insincere who makes a show of willing what he wills not. Now, whoever approaches Baptism, by that very fact makes a show of having right faith in Christ, of veneration for this sacrament, and of wishing to conform to the Church, and to renounce sin. Consequently, to whatever sin

---

[11] Joseph Cardinal Ratzinger, "The Pastoral Approach to Marriage Should be Founded on the Truth," footnote 4, *L'Osservatore Romano*, November 30, 2011.

a man wishes to cleave, if he approach Baptism, he approaches insincerely, which is the same as to approach without devotion.[12]

In real life, insincerity can sometimes manifest in dramatic ways. Rod Bennett, who entered the Church with his wife in 1996, tells this story:

> We had a guy who actually got up during the Mystagogia (having already received all three sacraments of initiation) and thanked the leaders for NOT converting him! He frankly admitted that the whole thing had been his girlfriend's idea, just to get married in the Church, and — happily — we had been willing to meet him halfway by assigning him a sponsor who had promised not to trouble him with anything "Catholic." During the small-group discussion time, for example, "We just sat and talked football," he beamed. The RCIA director watched approvingly during this little speech, apparently happy to have been of service!

While few of us have encountered such jaw-dropping candor, most leaders involved in sacramental prep and RCIA have had to wrestle with conflicts between individual and family expectations and whether or not someone is spiritually ready to receive *both* the sacrament and the sacramental grace in question. There are two common maxims that pastoral leaders often evoke as solutions in these

---

[12] Aquinas, *Summa Theologiae*, III, q69, a9, ad3.

situations. One is "The sacrament will take care of it," and the other that "The Church will provide."

"THE SACRAMENT WILL TAKE CARE OF IT"

Ralph Martin, director of graduate theology programs in evangelization at Sacred Heart Major Seminary, has often encountered the first maxim while working with Catholics around the globe for the past forty years:

> In contemporary sacramental practice one often hears that even though there appear to be serious defects of intention and preparation in someone who is approaching a sacrament, "The sacrament will take care of it."[13]

An experienced DRE friend pointed out that people in ministry seldom talk about the effects of the sacraments and rather tend to *assume* that individuals receive what the sacrament is supposed to offer. She noticed a widespread underlying misconception: "If we don't touch people in preparing them for the reception of the sacrament, then they will get it from the sacrament itself." The message is clear: those involved in sacramental prep do not have to worry when there is no obvious or overt sign that adults or teens are ready.

Karl Rahner wrote very directly about this common pastoral assumption:

---

[13] Martin, *The Post Christendom Sacramental Crisis.*

We must not be content casuistically to determine the minimum disposition for the various sacraments and so encourage the prejudice that the sacrament does the rest, or does so if received with maximum frequency (Eucharist, sacrament of Penance). It is meaningless to increase the frequency with which a sacrament is received if there is no growth in the personal moral participation by the individual in the accomplishment of the sacrament, i.e., in his disposition.[14]

The conviction that the "sacrament will take care of it" can arise from confusion about two different ways in which the word *faith* is used with reference to the sacraments. As I have noted before, Blessed John Paul II wrote about baptized Christians who were "still without any explicit personal attachment to Jesus Christ; they only have *the capacity to believe* placed within them by Baptism and the presence of the Holy Spirit."[15] The pope was reflecting a long-standing theological distinction that we don't usually make in English.

We often use the single English word *faith* to denote what is covered by two different Latin terms. The first Latin term, *virtus fidei*, means "the virtue of faith," which is the power or capacity to believe but *not* the act of faith itself. *Virtus fidei* is the sort of faith that Blessed John Paul II was referring to when he wrote of the "capacity to believe"

---

[14] "Disposition," *Encyclopedia of Theology: The Concise Sacramentum Mundi*, Karl Rahner, ed. (Freiburg-im-Breisgau: Herder KG, 1975), p. 352.

[15] Pope John Paul II, *Catechesi Tradendae*, 19, emphasis added.

placed within us by baptism that can exist without explicit personal attachment to Jesus Christ.

The Church uses a different term, *actus fidei*, for the explicit, personal act of faith that is at the heart of discipleship:

> The Catholic tradition holds that it is the virtue of faith that is bestowed in baptism. For that virtue to become a personal act of faith, it must be activated freely, explicitly, however minimally.... It is that personal act of faith, however minimal, and always under the grace of God, that transforms the human being from one who can be a believer into one who is a believer.... It is that act of faith that is required for right sacramental intention.[16]

The *virtus fidei*, the "capacity to believe" bestowed upon an infant at baptism, must become *actus fidei*, explicit personal faith, for a teen or adult to receive a sacrament fruitfully.

The Church's understanding of saving faith is that it is not merely the passive capacity for grace, which is part of human nature. Neither can true faith exist without charity. Intellectual assent to the doctrines of the Catholic faith *alone, without charity and good works*, is what the Church calls *fides informis*; it is a "dead" faith that does not save (James 2:18–26). True faith — the faith of a disciple — is faith that is infused with hope and love. As St. Paul says, "So faith, hope, love abide, these three; but the greatest of these

---

[16] Lawler, *Marriage and the Catholic Church*, pp. 54-55.

is love" (1 Corinthians 13:13). It is this living faith that the *United States Catholic Catechism for Adults* describes:

> Faith is first of all a personal adherence ... to God. At the same time, it is a free assent to the whole truth that God has revealed (CCC, no. 150). A personal faith says, "I believe in God."[17]

"The Church Will Provide"

The second maxim, "The Church will provide" (*ecclesia supplet*), is true, but it does *not* mean that the Church will "cover for us" if we don't possess genuine faith and spiritual openness to the grace being offered. *Ecclesia supplet* means that the Church, out of her treasury of grace, *may* compensate for the sacramental and liturgical mistakes of priests who intend to do what the Church intends.[18] But the Church has never taught that she would automatically supply the response of personal faith and obedience that only you and I can make.

What happens if we receive without personal faith? Father Raniero Cantalamessa, the preacher to the papal household, points out that when someone receives without proper disposition, the grace of God can be "tied":

> Catholic theology recognizes the concept of a valid but "tied" sacrament. A sacrament is called

---

17 *United States Catholic Catechism for Adults* (Washington, DC: USCCB Communications, 2006), p. 37.
18 James Bretzke, S.J., *Consecrated Phrases: A Latin Theological Dictionary* (Collegeville, MN: Liturgical Press, 1998), pp. 42-43.

tied if the fruit that should accompany it remains bound because of certain blocks that prevent its effectiveness.

In ... Baptism what is it that causes the fruit of the sacrament to stay tied? ... What does the *opus operantis* in Baptism — namely, man's part, consist of? It consists of faith! "Whoever believes and is baptized shall be saved" (Mk 16:16).[19]

The Council of Trent wrestled with the relationship of personal faith and grace in response to the challenge of the Protestant Reformers. Chapters 4 through 6 of the council's *Decree on Justification* describe in great detail the sort of spiritual development that needs to be in place in order for an adult to receive baptism fruitfully. It includes the following:

• Being moved to faith by hearing the basic proclamation of Jesus Christ and his work of salvation.
• Moving intentionally toward God.
• Believing in what God has revealed — especially that God saves sinners through redemption in Jesus Christ.
• Recognizing that one is a sinner.
• Trusting in the mercy of God.
• Beginning to hope in and to love God.
• Repenting of personal sin.

---

[19] Father Raniero Cantalamessa, O.F.M. Cap., "Baptism in the Holy Spirit," *International Catholic Charismatic Renewal Services Newsletter* (online at http://catholiccharismatic.us/ccc/articles/Cantalamessa/Cantalamessa_002.html, as of May 8, 2012).

- Resolving to be baptized, to begin a new life, and to walk in the obedience of faith.[20]

There is one obvious descriptor for someone who has lived all the above: *disciple*. What the council fathers were clearly saying is that an adult must "drop his or her nets" and begin the journey of intentional discipleship in order to receive baptism fruitfully.

Discipleship as the necessary minimum for baptism makes perfect sense when you contemplate what you are preparing to receive as an adult:

> The fruit of Baptism, or baptismal grace, is a rich reality that includes forgiveness of original sin and all personal sins, birth into the new life by which man becomes an adoptive son of the Father, a member of Christ and a temple of the Holy Spirit. By this very fact the person baptized is incorporated into the Church, the Body of Christ, and made a sharer in the priesthood of Christ. (CCC 1279)

COOPERATING GRACE

Raissa and Jacques Maritain entered the Church in 1906 from Jewish and Protestant backgrounds after a long and strenuous spiritual struggle. After their baptism, the Maritains became catalysts of a Catholic intellectual and cultural revival in France between the world wars. In her memoir, *We Have Been Friends Together*, Raissa describes the inten-

---

[20] Decree on Justification, Council of Trent, chapters 4–6.

sity of their preparation to love, serve, and obey God's leading immediately before their baptism:

> Once, during those months, I heard in my sleep
> these words, said to me with a certain impatience:
> "You are forever seeking what you must do. You
> have only to love God and serve Him with all your
> heart." Later I found these words in the *Imitation*,
> which I had not then read....

> Our suffering and dryness grew greater every day.
> Finally we understood that God also was waiting,
> and that there would be no further light so long as
> we should not have obeyed the imperious voice of
> our consciences saying to us: you have no valid ob-
> jection to the Church; she alone promises you the
> light of truth — prove her promises, put Baptism
> to the test.[21]

The Church has a remarkable term, "cooperating grace,"
for the process whereby we choose our spiritual destiny by
freely cooperating with God's initiative. God first gives us
the necessary "prevenient" grace to enable us to respond
to his initiative toward us. But we are under no compul-
sion; we still freely choose to obey. And then the Creator
and Lord of the universe, stunningly, chooses to "cooperate" with our choice. St. Thomas, quoting St. Augustine,
explains it this way:

---

[21] Raissa Maritain, *We Have Been Friends Together* (New York: Longmans,
Green, and Co., Inc., 1945), p. 175.

Augustine subjoins: "He operates that we may will; and when we will, He cooperates that we may perfect" (*De Gratia et Lib. Arbit.* Xvii).

> One thing is said to cooperate with another not merely when it is a secondary agent under a principal agent, but when it helps to the end intended. Now man is helped by God to will the good, through the means of operating grace. And hence, the end being already intended, grace cooperates with us.[22]

Of course, our personal response at the moment of receiving baptism or another sacrament is only the beginning of a lifetime of responding in faith to God's grace. If we don't intentionally seek to continue to grow in our faith, the initial grace we received can be thwarted. As part of our lifelong freedom, we retain — mysteriously and tragically — the power to "baffle" God's grace:

> That greater or lesser grace appears in the baptized may occur in two ways. First, because one receives greater grace in Baptism than another, on account of his greater devotion, as stated above. Secondly, because, though they receive equal grace, they do not make an equal use of it, but one applies himself more to advance therein, while another by his negligence baffles grace.[23]

---

[22] Aquinas, *Summa Theologiae*, I-II, q111, a2, ad3.
[23] Ibid., III, q69, a8, ad2.

Even in the case of small children, the graces received without obstacles in infant baptism must eventually unfold, develop, and "flower" in freely chosen personal growth (CCC 1231). Parents, godparents, and the whole Christian community play a huge role in intentionally fostering this spiritual development (CCC 1255), but the final choice must be made by the baptized person as a teen or adult. Since that is the case, how we help teens and adults prepare their hearts, minds, and souls to *receive* the grace of God fruitfully and then cooperate with that grace throughout life is every bit as crucial to the life and mission of the Church as making the sacraments available in the first place.

SOURCE AND SUMMIT

I have wondered if our sometimes casual talk about the Eucharist as "the source and summit of the Christian life"[24] is not distorted by the fact that most of the people doing the talking don't live around *serious* summits. My city, Colorado Springs, lies at the foot of the most famous mountain in the United States. Locals know that the song "America the Beautiful" was written about the view from the 14,115-foot-high pinnacle of Pike's Peak. They also know that the Barr Trail up Pike's Peak has the greatest elevation gain in a state famous for its rugged heights.

A small child could be carried up Pike's Peak, but adults cannot simply wander up to the summit casually, much less passively. They have to spend some seriously strenu-

---

[24] *Lumen Gentium*, 11.

ous hours covering nearly thirteen miles. They first ascend nearly five thousand feet through the foothills, the montane (forest), and then the sub-alpine climate zones, before climbing another three thousand feet beyond the tree line. A well-conditioned adult who is acclimated to the elevation can climb the Barr Trail in about thirteen hours. An extremely fit and fast man can run to the summit in just over two hours — but only if he has trained rigorously for months and even years beforehand. Part of the difficulty lies in the fact that the air at the top of Pikes Peak has 40 percent less oxygen than the air at sea level. You can't even drive to the summit of Pike's Peak casually, because there are long, twisty stretches with steep drop-offs but no guardrails. I speak from experience when I say that even passengers can't relax! One is too busy willing the car away from the edge of those magnificent thousand-foot drop-offs!

I don't think it is an accident that the Church uses the metaphor of a *summit* to convey the significance of the Eucharist.[25] The Eucharist is described as the summit, the apex, and the pinnacle of the Christian life because it contains "the whole spiritual good of the Church, namely Christ himself, our Pasch" (CCC 1324). Just as we have to actively climb a mountain summit, we have to make an intentional journey, properly prepared, to fully receive the inexhaustible grace to be found in the Eucharistic Christ.

This is why the Church specifies that the liturgy "must be preceded by evangelization, faith, and conversion" (CCC 1072) in order for adults to experience the intended fruits of the Mass. The Mass is designed to nourish the spiritual

---

[25] Ibid.

lives of those who have *already* made the decision to follow Jesus Christ up the foothills and through the forests of personal faith and discipleship.

> But in order that the liturgy may be able to produce its full effects, it is necessary that the faithful come to it with proper dispositions, that their minds should be attuned to their voices, and that they should cooperate with divine grace lest they receive it in vain [cf. 2 Cor. 6:1]. Pastors of souls must therefore realize that, when the liturgy is celebrated, something more is required than the mere observation of the laws governing valid and licit celebration; it is their duty also to ensure that the faithful take part fully aware of what they are doing, actively engaged in the rite, and enriched by its effects.[26]

The general principle at work is always that "*those who want more of the Lord will receive more of the Lord.*"[27] This is why the Mass requires the "conscious, active, and fruitful participation" of all present.[28]

---

[26] *Sacrosanctum Concilium* (Constitution on the Sacred Liturgy), 11 (available online at http://www.vatican.va/archive/hist_councils/ii_vatican_council/documents/vat-ii_const_19631204_sacrosanctum-concilium_en.html, as of May 8, 2012).

[27] Ralph Martin, "A New Pentecost? Catholic Theology and Baptism in the Spirit," *Logos*, Vol. 14:3, Summer 2011.

[28] Pope John Paul II, *Ecclesia de Eucharistia* (On the Eucharist and Its Relationship to the Church), 10 (online at http://www.vatican.va/holy_father/special_features/encyclicals/documents/hf_jp-ii_enc_20030417_ecclesia_eucharistia_en.html, as of May 8, 2012).

WITH FEAR AND TREMBLING STAND

The consequences of receiving the sacraments without faith, of receiving in vain, are not merely that nothing happens and that therefore we just "don't get the good stuff." On the contrary, we can actually *hurt* ourselves by receiving in vain. Most practicing Catholics are aware that one way that we can seriously hurt ourselves is by receiving Communion in a state of unconfessed mortal sin, which is sacrilege:

> Just as Christ's Passion has not its effect in them who are not disposed towards it as they should be, so also they do not come to glory through this sacrament who receive it unworthily. Hence Augustine (Tract. xxvi in Joan.), expounding the same passage, observes: "The sacrament is one thing, the power of the sacrament another. Many receive it from the altar … and by receiving" … die…. Eat, then, spiritually the heavenly "bread, bring innocence to the altar." It is no wonder, then, if those who do not keep innocence, do not secure the effect of this sacrament.[29]

But receiving fruitfully requires that we not only be in a state of grace but also have a "right," or supernatural, intention. To benefit from receiving Communion, our intention must be to please God, to be more closely united with him, to gain a remedy for our weaknesses. In other words, we must already be in a conscious, personal relationship with

---

[29] Aquinas, *Summa Theologiae*, III, q79, a2, ad2, quoting Augustine, (Tract. xxvi in Joan.).

God and desire to become ever closer. To reap the fullest benefits, we should also be free from all attachment to anything sinful.[30]

But in fact, *mere carelessness, lack of preparation, or lack of thanksgiving can also be harmful.* Pope John Paul II, in his very first encyclical, wrote that if one does not constantly try to grow spiritually, receiving the Eucharist will lack its full redeeming effectiveness, and there can even be a spiritual loss.[31] Father William G. Most observed that to receive Communion out of mere routine, with no special care, no thanksgiving, is more apt to cause spiritual loss than gain.[32]

Maurice De La Taille, S.J., summed up the Church's teaching in 1921 with language that still resonates powerfully with Catholics who are familiar with J. R. R. Tolkien's *The Lord of the Rings.* Tolkien was a devout Catholic with a great devotion to the Eucharist. Picture Frodo and Sam on their long, extraordinary journey across Middle Earth and, at last, making the final ascent of Mount Doom, and then read Father Taille's words: *"The faithful in this life obtain the fruit of the Mass … by way of personal quest."*[33]

---

[30] Father William G. Most, *A Basic Catholic Catechism*, 1990, part 12, Holy Communion (available online at www.ewtn.com/library/CATECHSM/MOSTCAT.htm, as of May 8, 2012).

[31] Pope John Paul II, *Redemptor Hominis* ("The Redeemer of Man"), 20 (online at http://www.vatican.va/holy_father/john_paul_ii/encyclicals/documents/hf_jp-ii_enc_04031979_redemptor-hominis_en.html, as of May 8, 2012).

[32] Most, *A Basic Catholic Catechism*, part 12, Holy Communion.

[33] Maurice De La Taille, S.J., *The Mystery of Faith: Regarding the Most August Sacrament and Sacrifice of the Body and Blood of Christ*, Thesis XXIX, 1921, emphasis added (online at www.ewtn.com/library/theology/myoffait.htm, as of May 8, 2012).

In the twenty-first century, we know "Let All Mortal Flesh Keep Silence" as one of the most ancient of Christmas carols. Ancient it is, but a carol it most certainly is not. It was written seventeen centuries ago as a Greek chant of Eucharistic devotion within the Liturgy of St. James. Read the powerful words of this chant with the Eucharist in mind (or better still, in the presence of the Eucharist):

> Let all mortal flesh keep silence,
> And with fear and trembling stand;
> Ponder nothing earthly minded,
> For with blessing in his hand,
> Christ our God to earth descendeth,
> Our full homage to demand.
>
> King of kings, yet born of Mary,
> As of old on earth he stood,
> Lord of lords, in human vesture,
> In the body and the blood;
> He will give to all the faithful
> His own self for heavenly food.
>
> Rank on rank the host of heaven
> Spreads its vanguard on the way,
> As the Light of light descendeth
> From the realms of endless day,
> That the powers of hell may vanish
> As the darkness clears away.
>
> At his feet the six-winged seraph,
> Cherubim with sleepless eye,
> Veil their faces to the presence,

As with ceaseless voice they cry:
Alleluia, Alleluia,
Alleluia, Lord Most High!

Nothing could be further from the numb, bored passivity with which many of us, myself included, have often routinely received the Eucharist.

The spiritual realities that we are only faintly aware of now will be revealed in all their fullness at the end of our lives. Christ will reveal the "secret disposition" of our hearts and reward us according to our personal "acceptance or refusal of grace" (CCC 682).

Given that the majority of baptized Catholics do not even attend Mass on a regular basis, I think we may safely question whether many Catholic adults possess the inner disposition of discipleship necessary for the sacraments, *as well as liturgical and personal prayer*, to have their intended effect and bear their intended fruit. The vast majority of Catholics have received the sacraments validly and have received the character — if a character is involved — but we must ask whether they have also received, or received fully, the "inward reality."

Our failure to evangelize our own has profound implications for the ultimate eternal destiny of each person and for the Church's mission and world's life. For the immersion into the life, death, and mission of Christ intended to occur at baptism is not only our hope for our eternal salvation; it is also the source for all ecclesial and secular vocations. The grace of baptism includes all the baptized in the priestly, prophetic, and kingly offices of Christ, making them participants in the mission of the whole Christian people for the sake of the world. All the baptized are to be "anointed" ones, little "Christs" who share in the same mission of Jesus the Christ as "priests" and temples of the Holy Spirit. It is no accident that Jesus speaks of discipleship as preceding baptism in what many Christians know as "The Great Commission":

> Go therefore and make *disciples* of all nations, baptizing them in the name of the Father and of the Son and of the Holy Spirit, teaching them to observe all that I have commanded you; and behold, I am with you always, to the close of the age. (Matthew 28:19–20, emphasis added)

SEEKING REVIVAL

Even if we were not ready to receive them fruitfully when they were conferred, the graces poured out on us in baptism, confirmation, and holy orders are not lost. Sacraments that bestow a character can be "revived" when the recipient comes to personal faith, repents, and chooses to follow Jesus Christ as a disciple in the midst of his Church. This fact is the "secret" behind the tremendous impact that evangelizing retreats like Cursillo, Christ Renews His Parish, and Life in the Spirit Seminars have had on the lives of millions of Catholics over the past seventy years. In our travels, we have met thousands of lifelong Catholics whose faith, lives, and priorities were utterly transformed when they responded to an explicit call to discipleship.

> Renewing Christian initiation in adults — its effec-
> tiveness in reactivating Baptism consists in this: fi-
> nally man contributes his part — namely, he makes
> a choice of faith, prepared in repentance that allows
> the work of God to set itself free and to emanate
> all its strength.... The gift of God is finally "untied"
> and the Spirit is allowed to flow like a fragrance in
> the Christian life.[34]

Catholics often begin to get nervous at this point in the discussion, concerned that any talk of conversion or disposition must inevitably lead to a spiritual "inquisition" in which the "converted" eagerly sit in judgment of everybody else. But there is simply no basis for such judgments. Jesus tells us not to judge one another for the simple reason that *we don't know* what's going on in our neighbor's heart. You and I have no right to judge another's internal disposition, nor can we see justification happen in an individual's soul.

But this does not mean that *no* fruits of personal faith are observable from the outside. And it certainly does not mean that a dramatic and widespread absence of these fruits in the community overall cannot be recognized and addressed. Nor does it mean that we shouldn't talk about these realities and structure our pastoral priorities and practices around doing everything we can to foster positive disposition and the fruit that flows from it.

In calling Catholics to a deliberate discipleship and intentional faith, our goal is not to create a community of spiritual elites. Rather it is to create *a spiritual culture that*

---

[34] Cantalamessa, "Baptism in the Holy Spirit."

recognizes, openly talks about, and honors both the inward and outward dimensions of the sacraments and the liturgy. The Lord who said, "By this my Father is glorified, that you bear much fruit, and so prove to be my disciples" (John 15:8), urges us to build a community that fosters disciples, encourages all the baptized to bear fruit, and is structured to help all the baptized to become open to and receive God's grace in all its fullness. Our goal must be to help anyone who is open to develop a positive inward disposition that runs to do God's will and results in abundant and amazing fruit for the sake of the Church and the world.

Given what we know about the current state of discipleship and impoverishment of sacramental faith, the question is, "Now what? Can we turn this situation around?" How can we intentionally call postmodern people to follow Jesus — the heart of positive disposition — in the midst of his Church? How can we deliberately and effectively help ordinary Catholics in the pew make the journey to intentional discipleship?

CHAPTER 5

Thresholds of Conversion: Can I Trust You?

Peter Parker: "You don't trust anyone, that's your problem."

J. Jonah Jameson: "I trust my barber."

SPIDER-MAN (FILM)

W here do we start when seeking to make disciples of unevangelized Catholics? Let us get a common assumption out of the way first. With most twenty-first-century people (there are always exceptions), we can't *start* with catechesis. They aren't ready for it yet, and if they aren't ready, it will just roll off like water off a duck's back. In any case, catechesis is designed to foster the maturation of disciples, not the initial conversion of those who aren't yet disciples:

> The aim of catechesis is to be the teaching and maturation stage ... the period in which the Christian, having accepted by faith the person of Jesus Christ as the one Lord and having given Him complete adherence by sincere conversion of heart, endeavors to know better this Jesus to whom he has entrusted himself.[1]

---

[1] Pope John Paul II, *Catechesi Tradendae*, 20, emphasis added.

125

The *National Directory for Catechesis* outlines two critical steps that should precede catechesis: pre-evangelization and initial proclamation of the basic kerygma, or the Great Story of Jesus Christ.[2] Both are necessary to awaken initial Christian faith, and as we have seen, Christian faith is necessary for catechesis to be fruitful.

Catholic pastoral practice has few structures for these two preliminary stages. We typically presume that pre-evangelization and initial proclamation just happen automatically during basic catechesis. All the evidence suggests that even if true evangelization once worked that way, it is not working that way anymore. Catechized Catholics are clearly not necessarily evangelized Catholics.

I've listened to hundreds of Catholic leaders lament the failure of catechesis since Vatican II. So often we talk as if our problems would be over if we could just convey the concepts and facts of the faith to people accurately enough. A failure of catechesis may have been a major factor in the 1960s, but we are now two generations past the council. The situation in the West today is far beyond a failure of catechesis.

Today we can presume hardly anything about an individual's true beliefs and lived spiritual experience even when we are dealing with a baptized Catholic who attended CCD classes or received a Catholic education. Catechesis remains hugely important, especially for those on the verge of discipleship and afterward, but *not as a starting place* when evangelizing in the twenty-first-century West.

---

[2]   United States Conference of Catholic Bishops, Department of Communications, *National Directory for Catechesis* (Washington, DC: USCCB Publishing, 2005) p. 49.

In the mid-1990s, a campus minister named Doug Schaupp was struggling with similar problems. He and his ministry team at UCLA realized that "students weren't responding in the same ways they had before. Sharing the truth of Jesus' gospel no longer moved people. Our evangelistic labors resonated less, and had less fruit."[3]

During the 1997–1998 school year, thirty-seven students went through conversion experiences. Schaupp's team responded by doing something unusual. They asked these students to describe their spiritual journeys:

> At the end of the year, we interviewed most of the 37 students to find out what kind of internal and external dynamics helped them into the Kingdom of God. What we found was that they actually all went through the same phases of growth and transformation, though each student obviously took different amounts of time to grow from one place to the next.[4]

What they discovered was remarkable. First, Schaupp and his collaborators found that all thirty-seven students passed through a series of thresholds or stages of conversion — five in all — that culminated in a commitment to follow Jesus Christ as a disciple. Each transition to a new threshold was a genuine work of grace, empowered by the Holy Spirit, but each threshold also required real spiritual

---

[3] Don Everts and Doug Schaupp, *I Once Was Lost: What Postmodern Skeptics Taught Us About Their Path to Jesus* (Downers Grove, IL: IVP, 2008), pp. 12-13.

[4] Doug Schaupp, "Five Thresholds of Postmodern Conversion" (online at www.intervarsity.org/evangelism/article_item.php?article_id=1505, as of May 8, 2012).

energy and real choices on the part of the person making the journey. Conversion didn't "just happen" for these young adults. It required their ever-increasing commitment to more and more profound choices. After spending ten years walking with another 2,000 students on the journey to discipleship, Schaupp and co-author, Don Everts, wrote a book about their discoveries.[5]

What they "discovered" was as ancient and perennial as the journey taken by the blind man in John 9:1–38, who went through a series of steps on his way to full commitment to Jesus. When first questioned, he spoke of "the man called Jesus" (v. 11). Then he described Jesus as a prophet (v. 17). Then he acknowledged him as "from God" (v. 33). Finally, he called him "Lord" and "he worshiped him" (v. 38).

THE FIVE THRESHOLDS OF CONVERSION

When I first stumbled across a draft of Schaupp's initial paper on the thresholds eight years ago, I instantly sensed that here was a language for something that nearly everyone in pastoral ministry has encountered. We all know lots of Catholics who have some genuine spiritual yearnings — Catholics in whom the Holy Spirit is obviously at work — and yet who are clearly not yet disciples or even close to discipleship. Listening to people's journeys in light of these thresholds or stages of conversion enables us to honor the first reality while dealing effectively with the second.

Keep in mind that the thresholds are strictly focused upon one's lived relationship with God rather than one's

---

[5]   Everts and Schaupp, *I Once Was Lost.*

baptismal status or knowledge of the faith. One of the fascinating things you learn as you listen is that some baptized and catechized Catholics have not even progressed as far as simple trust (the first threshold), while some of the unbaptized are much further along the road. A few may even be intentional disciples without having yet been baptized.

Our maxim has become "Never accept a label in place of a story." For postmoderns, common spiritual labels like "Catholic" and "agnostic" are as likely to hide reality as to reveal it. There is no way of knowing what a particular person's journey has truly been and where the person is now until we earn the right to hear his or her story and then listen carefully and prayerfully.

Let's look at these five thresholds briefly and then zero in on the first threshold in more detail. (We have adapted the language slightly to better fit a Catholic context.):

1. **Initial trust:** A person is able to *trust* or has a positive association with Jesus Christ, the Church, a Christian believer, or something identifiably Christian. Trust is *not* the same as active personal faith. Without some kind of bridge of trust in place, people will not move closer to God.

2. **Spiritual curiosity:** A person finds himself *intrigued* by or desiring to know more about Jesus, his life, and his teachings or some aspect of the Christian faith. This curiosity can range from mere awareness of a new possibility to something quite intense. Nevertheless, a person at the threshold of curiosity is not yet open to personal change. Curiosity is still essentially passive, but it is more than mere trust.

3. **Spiritual openness:** A person acknowledges to himself or herself and to God that he or she is open to the *possibility* of personal and spiritual change. This is one of the most difficult transitions for a postmodern nonbeliever. Openness is not a commitment to change. People who are open are simply admitting they are *open to the possibility* of change.

4. **Spiritual seeking:** The person moves from being essentially passive to actively seeking to know the God who is calling him or her. It is, if you will, "dating with a purpose" but not yet marriage. Seekers are asking, "Are you the one to whom I will give myself?" At this stage, the seeker is engaged in an urgent spiritual quest, seeking to know whether he or she can commit to Christ in his Church.

5. **Intentional discipleship:** This is the decision to "drop one's nets," to make a conscious commitment to follow Jesus in the midst of his Church as an obedient disciple and to reorder one's life accordingly.

INSIDE AND OUTSIDE

It is important for those who are committed Catholics — especially those who have never known anything else — to remember that a threshold usually looks and feels very different to "insiders" than it does to someone approaching from the outside. As evangelizers, we need to make a real effort to imagine; to see Christ, the faith, and the Church through the eyes of outsiders. The same threshold can seem overwhelming and insurmountable to them while looking very simple and obvious to us.

One important side note: We have found that people who are already disciples within another Christian tradition usually go through these same stages as they contemplate the possibility of entering the Catholic Church. This was certainly true for me when I first considered entering the Church. I had been raised as a strongly anti-Catholic fundamentalist in southern Mississippi, and contemplating becoming Catholic was like considering becoming a Martian.

I brought a big book about Catholicism to my first RCIA session. In those days, I was completely clueless about intra-Catholic squabbles and presumed that all books on Catholicism came from the same basic perspective. I put my big book underneath my battered metal chair and waited for the session to begin. A member of the RCIA team sat down next to me, glanced at the title of my book, and fixed me with a knowing look. "I see where you're coming from," he said.

"What?" I was completely mystified. "*I* don't even know where I'm coming from. How do *you* know where I'm coming from?"

That was my first clue that there were mysteries involved in being Catholic that weren't covered in the *Catechism*.

It's a Mystery

There is no one-size-fits-all way of negotiating the journey to discipleship. People will move through at different paces. In intense retreat settings, some may bound through a couple thresholds in a few days. Others may stay stuck in one place for years or ping-pong back and forth between different thresholds. There may be great leaps forward as well as relapses to earlier thresholds.

The thing to remember is that we are not in control of this process. Some people will not respond to our best efforts to be helpful. Jesus warned us that some people will not receive the "seed" (Mark 4:14–19). Others may dazzle us by choosing to cooperate with grace and become the good soil that brings forth thirty, sixty, and a hundredfold. We are dealing with the mystery of a relationship that God himself is initiating in the human heart.

Let me stress that *we* cannot bring anyone to faith through pressure, guilt, argument, or cleverness. Conversion and true faith are works of the Holy Spirit. But it is also true that we can, by our responses, help or hinder another's journey. Responding to seekers in a way that does not accept and honor their lived experience may cause them to "freeze" or even move away from God. Understanding the thresholds can help us help them or, at least, help us to not get in the way of what God is doing.

THE FIRST THRESHOLD: TRUST

What do we mean by *trust* in this context?

The threshold of trust is not the same as active personal faith. *Trust*, in this case, refers just to a basic, *felt* trust of something or someone associated with Christ or the Church. What this means can vary widely.

A dear friend of mine, raised in a completely nonreligious household, somehow came to the conclusion that Christmas wasn't Christmas if he hadn't heard Linus recite the Nativity story from the Gospel of Luke in *A Charlie Brown Christmas*. He trusted in the goodness of that story, though he didn't learn anything else about Christianity for many years. A cartoon was his initial bridge of trust.

Another close friend lives in the Persian Gulf, speaks Arabic fluently, and often goes places few Western women ever visit. She has lived for twenty-five years in a Muslim context in order to be a living witness to Jesus and his Kingdom. She has become friends with a Sudanese Muslim who had a wonderful experience as a student at a Catholic girls' school. Her experience in that Catholic school was her bridge of trust. It disposed her to trust a Western Christian like my friend.

The first task of evangelization is to find out if a bridge of trust already exists. Does our friend or colleague or roommate or family member *trust* or have some kind of positive association with Jesus Christ, the Church, a believer, or something identifiably Christian? If this trust does not already exist, then our first job as an evangelizer is to help build that bridge.

This is especially vital now that a fundamental distrust of Christianity in general and the Catholic Church in particular is the new normal in many places. After a decade of scandal, Catholics must work hard to earn trust — in some parts of the country and in some situations more than others. Where trust has been severely violated, it can be difficult to build or restore. Although effective Catholic media can help, we earn such trust primarily through relationships: through the integrity, compassion, warmth, and joy of our own life and faith. Even excellent Catholic media often do not have the impact of a radiant personal witness.

Most active Catholics are at least at the threshold of trust. Many nonpracticing Catholics and "former" Catholics do not have a bridge of trust in place, which would enable them to retrace their steps. As we work to rebuild trust or to build it for the first time, we must pray and work to avoid the natural reactions to the distrust directed at us. We need to avoid such things as defensiveness, seeing ourselves as a "victim," and avoiding or judging those who don't trust us.

TRUST CAN BE COMPLICATED

The vast majority of Catholics who attend Mass regularly do possess a basic trust, but a surprising question remains: In whom or what are they trusting? What active Christians trust and distrust may surprise you.

I once did a gifts-discernment interview with a man who was a pillar of his parish. He was a leader in youth ministry and active in online apologetics. By any standard, he was what the demographers call an "active Catholic." He was a lovely, warm man who lit up when he talked about his kids and family. But when I asked this man to describe his relationship with God, his affect changed so dramatically that it was almost like a blow. His whole body became rigid, and he scowled as he said, "I think of God as a horrible, destructive being. If I don't ask him for anything in this life, he may let me through in the end." When I recovered from my surprise, I asked him why he did Internet apologetics if he felt that way. "Oh, I trust the Church," he responded. "I just don't trust God."

Though he was grappling with a radically defective mental and emotional picture of God, he trusted the people of the Church and so he stayed. He was still there because there was a bridge of trust. On the other hand, I've told that story to many people, and the majority snort and say, "I'm the opposite. I trust God, but I don't trust the Church." Distrust can take startling forms. At one of our conferences, I met a Catholic woman who had a great devotion to the Virgin Mary but did not trust any member of the Trinity or the Church.

Many don't trust God or the Church, but they do trust a Christian in their life. Maybe they trust you. *You* may be the bridge that one day will lead them to a life-changing encounter with Christ.

For someone at this very early threshold, it is far more important that trust exist than that it make theological sense. Our job at this point is to affirm, strengthen, and if possible broaden whatever trust exists.

WE WILL NEVER EVANGELIZE
WHAT WE DO NOT LOVE

As we know, the majority of Gen X and Millennial Catholics do not attend Mass. They are not coming to us, so we will have to go to them. But who will do so?

> For the clergy it is easier to be pastors than to be fishermen — that is, it is easier to nourish those who come to the Church through the word and the sacraments than it is to seek out those who are far off in cultural environments that are very different. The parable of the lost sheep is reversed today: ninety-nine sheep have gone off and one remains in the sheepfold. The danger for us is to spend all our time nourishing this one remaining sheep and not to have time — also because of the scarcity of clergy — to seek out those who are lost. The contribution of the laity in this situation seems providential.[6]

An exceedingly bright twenty-five-year-old Catholic, with a love for the traditional liturgy *and* a passion for evangelization, put his finger on a very real problem for me a couple of years ago. He observed, "My generation of Cath-

---

[6] "Father Cantalamessa on Christ Yesterday and Today (Part I)," Zenit, December 2, 2005 (online at www.zenit.org/article-14723?l=english, as of May 8, 2012).

olics isn't prepared to evangelize my generation, are we?" There is a vast gap in worldview and sensibilities between the majority of practicing Millennials and the rest of their generation — the 80 percent who are largely missing in action. Scott McKnight, writing in *Leadership Journal*, noted:

> Many emerging adults have been reared into a world vastly different than the self-esteem culture. Some gravitate, instead, toward an Augustinian perception of the self and find their own contemporaries annoying.[7]

As one serious young Catholic man put it:

> I'm twenty-three, and I'd hardly call myself immune from the rampant idiocies of my generation, but this may actually explain why I find so many of my peers illogical and infuriating when it comes to moral issues. It's like we are speaking entirely different languages.[8]

Each generation is largely responsible for the evangelization of its own. But trust cannot be built if the evangelizers regard the unevangelized with fear and disdain. Francis Cardinal George of Chicago summed up our dilemma brilliantly years ago: "We will never evangelize what we do not love."

---

[7] Scott McKnight, "The Gospel for iGens," *Leadership Journal*, September 14, 2009 (online at www.christianitytoday.com/le/2009/summer/thegospelforigens.html?start=3, as of May 8, 2012).

[8] Sherry Weddell, *American Catholicism: Living on the Edge of a Demographic Precipice* (online at www.siena.org/December-2010/living-in-the-land-of-qnoneq, as of May 8, 2012).

When I occasionally hear Catholics talk hopefully (or gleefully!) about certain groups of Catholics — whose theological or liturgical leanings they dislike — leaving the Church, I know that we cannot have grasped what is at stake. We cannot have grasped the nature of the immortal beings we are blithely hoping will leave the fullness of the means of grace. We must recognize that it is a form of profound disobedience for us to wish, in the name of purity, for what Christ himself prayed with great intensity would never happen: that he would lose one of those that his Father had given him (see John 17:11–19).

Granted, Pope Benedict referred to the possibility of a smaller Catholic Church before he became pope:

> Maybe we are facing a new and different kind of epoch in the Church's history, where Christianity will again be characterized more by the mustard seed, where it will exist in small, seemingly insignificant groups that nonetheless live an intense struggle against evil and bring good into the world — that let God in.[9]

But then-Cardinal Ratzinger was merely reading the signs of the times, recognizing that Christendom as it has existed for the past 1,200 years (as opposed to Christianity) is well and truly dead. The pope knows that the Church must look again, as she has in the past, not to institutions

---

9   Joseph Cardinal Ratzinger, *Salt of the Earth: The Church at the End of the Millennium — An Interview With Peter Seewald* (San Francisco: Ignatius Press, 1997), p. 16.

or societal favor but to the power of the Holy Spirit, the redeeming work of Christ, the truth of the apostolic faith, the deep personal faith of her people, profound prayer and worship, and the intercession of the communion of saints. She must also look to the charisms, vocations, saints, cultural creativity, and mighty deeds that arise out of such faith — the faith that gave birth to the structures and cultures of Western Christianity in the first place.

We should never, never cease to pray for, long for, labor for, and call every man and woman to encounter Christ in the midst of his Church. We can never accept, cooperate with, or most appallingly, rejoice in events and changes that endanger the eternal happiness of millions of those redeemed by Christ's sacrifice and baptized in Christ's name.

Evangelization isn't about us. It is about Jesus Christ, the Good Shepherd, seeking the lost sheep through us. When we forget that, we can alienate and even lose those whom God has called us to bring to Jesus. Raised as a "nothing," Sara Silberger paints a vivid picture of how generational tensions among the RCIA team looked to her as an outsider entering the Church:

> The "old hippies" were all trying to pull the candidates aside and explain to them how bad it was when everyone had to speak Latin, and when they were finished, the angry young men were waiting on the other side to pull the candidates aside and explain to them how the old hippies had ruined the music. I wish I could explain how disillusioning and ridiculous it all looks from the outside, and how much of

it makes literally no sense to someone like me who doesn't already have years of exposure to this stuff.[10]

Paul Wallace had a very different experience and describes the transforming power of the kind of love that builds trust and that changed his life:

I am not a Christian because it "makes sense" or because someone sat down and diagrammed it for me. I am a Christian because I have been loved deeply and unconditionally by Christians. Some of them … troubled me with hard questions. But all of them loved me when I did not love them…. Reason is a wonderful tool, but it is a weak force for deep change in human beings. Faith, hope, and love are not tools; they are virtues, powerful and exceedingly difficult to embody, and much more efficacious than reason for changing lives.[11]

Now let's take a look at the second threshold: curiosity.

---

[10] Sherry Weddell, *Unintentional Mega-Blogging: The Collapse of Cultural Catholicism* (online at www.siena.org/January-2011/unintentional-mega-blogging-the-collapse-of-cultural-catholicism, as of May 8, 2012).

[11] Paul Wallace, *Why I Am a Christian* (online at psnt.net/blog/2010/12/why-i-am-a-christian/, as of May 8, 2012).

CHAPTER 6

The Second Threshold: Curiosity

"Curiouser and curiouser!"

ALICE IN WONDERLAND (BOOK)

Once someone has a bridge of trust in place, our role as evangelizers is to help our friend move toward the spiritual threshold of *curiosity*. To be sure, spiritual curiosity and how it plays out in the lives of individuals can vary widely. One person is instinctively curious about the Church's philosophical or spiritual tradition, a second is intrigued by the inner peace of the Catholic woman he is dating, and a third is mysteriously moved by the rosary she found among her late grandmother's things. All these brushes with grace can be the beginning of a journey into the heart of the Catholic faith.

The first and most obvious question is "Curiosity about what?" The answer is that if our ultimate mission is to make disciples of Jesus Christ, our task at this stage in the journey is to first arouse curiosity about *Jesus Christ*. To do that, we have to *talk about Jesus*.

ABOUT JESUS HARDLY AT ALL

As we have seen, it is difficult to think about things you have never heard anyone else talk about. I have been part of many conversations about the Catholic discomfort at using the naked name of Jesus. We talk endlessly about the Church but so seldom about Christ as a person with whom we are in a relationship. Few things trigger the fear of being "Protestant" more quickly than naming the Name. A witty friend summed up this dynamic in a memorable way: Jesus is "He who must not be named."

Father Gregory Jensen is an Orthodox priest who knows that the Orthodox community struggles with the same dynamic:

> The more I follow the online discussions … the more I follow the debates and disagreements in the Church about administrative unity, or the concerns expressed about the moral or personal or administrative or leadership failings of the bishops or the clergy, the more I become convinced that whatever might be the truth of these concerns, ALL of this is simply a distraction. No, it's more than that. It's a justification, an excuse, for not helping each other and those outside the Church fall in love with Jesus Christ. How easy it is to talk about everything, but about Jesus hardly at all.[1]

There are other ways that we can distance ourselves from the person of Jesus. I once helped design an RCIA program with a group of friends. We thought it would be valuable and fun to let the group encounter Jesus directly by reading the Gospel of Luke together during inquiry. The

---

[1]   Father Gregory Jensen, "About Jesus Hardly at All" (online at palamas .info/?p=5857, as of May 8, 2012).

director of religious education with whom we were working disapproved and told us that we were "too Christocen-
tric." Over time it became clear that he was much more
comfortable dealing with Jesus Christ as a "topic" within
Catholicism. There was Jesus, the Trinity, the Church, the
Scriptures, Mary, the liturgy, the sacraments, the creed, social justice, and so on: all topics presented under the head-
ing of "Things Catholics Believe."

Whenever we treat Jesus as a "topic" within the faith
instead of as the "whole spiritual good of the Church"
(CCC 1324), or as a "belief" among other beliefs instead of
as Lord, Head, Bridegroom, Savior, and Elder Brother, we
profoundly distort the faith and communicate an impersonal or institutional understanding of what it means to be
Catholic. That is why the Church teaches:

> There is no true evangelization if the name, the
> teaching, the life, the promises, the kingdom and
> the mystery of Jesus of Nazareth, the Son of God,
> are not proclaimed.[2]

One very effective RCIA director summed up her mission this way: "My job in the inquiry period is to help people fall in love with Jesus. My job in the catechumenate is
to help people fall in love with the Church."

We must also talk about Jesus because we can no longer
presume solid knowledge of Jesus' life, death, and resurrection on the part of Catholics. For instance, a 2010 Barna

---

[2] Pope Paul VI, *Evangelii Nuntiandi* (On Evangelization in the Modern
World), 22 (online at http://www.vatican.va/holy_father/paul_vi/apost_
exhortations/documents/hf_p-vi_exh_19751208_evangelii-nuntiandi_
en.html, as of May 8, 2012).

Group study of American perceptions of Easter found that while the majority of Catholics understood Easter as a religious holiday (65 percent), only 37 percent (!) listed the Resurrection as the meaning of the day.[3] This is especially disturbing in light of the fact that Easter is the greatest of all feasts and one of the two times in the year when Catholic Mass attendance is at its highest (68 percent).[4] By comparison, Protestants were more likely than Catholics both to view Easter as a religious holiday and to connect the occasion to Jesus' rising from death (78 percent and 51 percent, respectively).

Former Catholics and nonbelievers of every stripe who are disdainful of Christianity often know very little about Jesus, and the little they think they know can be wrong. So they can be completely unprepared for the surprise of meeting him. The threshold of curiosity is a perfect time to explore the possibility that a personal God exists and that you can have a personal relationship with that God. It is essential that we help people wrestle with this first, most crucial issue of a personal God. *Those who don't believe in a personal God and the possibility of a relationship with that God will never be able to move beyond the threshold of curiosity.*

---

[3] The Barna Group, "Most Americans Consider Easter a Religious Holiday, But Fewer Correctly Identify Its Meaning," March 15, 2010 (online at www.barna.org/barna-update/article/13-culture/356-most-americans-consider-easter-a-religious-holiday-but-fewer-correctly-identify-its-meaning?q=easter, as of May 8, 2012).

[4] Mark Gray, "Catholics Come Home ... But Just For A Visit?" Nineteen Sixty-Four blog, Center for Applied Research in the Apostolate (CARA) (online at http://nineteensixty-four.blogspot.com/2011/11/catholics-come-home-but-just-for-visit.html, as of May 8, 2012).

At this stage, individuals often need a very safe, non-threatening way to express their curiosity without overreaction or pressure from us. It is very important that we tread lightly here. You can easily quench inquiries by drowning a teaspoon full of curiosity with a gallon of answers. Match your response to your friend's level of curiosity, and then wait for her to become curious again.

THE PEDAGOGY OF CURIOSITY

There are three basic stages of curiosity:

1. **Awareness:** This is the moment when people become aware that there are more possibilities in life than they had imagined or experienced. One such possibility could be "I can have a personal relationship with a God who loves me."
2. **Engagement:** This is when the curious person takes steps on his own to pursue his curiosity by, say, making friends with a Christian, reading about Jesus, and so on.
3. **Exchange:** The convert begins to experience intense curiosity. He moves from merely listening and semi-covert examination of Christians and their faith to actively asking questions and exchanging ideas. [5]

One of the best ways to rouse curiosity is to ask questions, not answer them. Catholic experience can make this difficult. English-speaking Catholic culture has been profoundly shaped by centuries of being a misunderstood religious minority in a hostile, largely Protestant world. In an environ-

---

[5] Everts and Schaupp, *I Once Was Lost*, p. 52.

ment filled with deeply embedded anti-Catholicism, Catholics naturally felt on the defensive, and training in apologetics was common in Catholic high schools and colleges. You had to be ready to defend the Church by explaining Catholic teaching and trying to correct the sometimes ludicrous misunderstandings of your non-Catholic friends and neighbors.

One of the funniest true stories I've ever heard is told by my friend Janet, whose mother trained as a hairdresser when she was young. In beauty school, the students would take turns doing one another's hair. When it came time for Jan's mom to play the customer, the classmate working on her hair asked suddenly, "Where are the horns?"

"Where are the *what*?"

"Well ... where are the horns?" her classmate asked again. "You're Catholic, aren't you?" This young woman was certain that Catholics had little horns on their heads that were cleverly hidden by their hair.

Our strong catechetical and apologetics instinct, while understandable, can get in the way of evangelizing postmodern people. Of course, there is a point at which basic catechesis becomes *very* important, but for most people that comes later in the journey. We are not, at this threshold, about the business of telling people *all* that the Church teaches. Rather, our goal is to arouse spiritual curiosity by our lives and by raising questions that pose the ultimate question: "Who do you think that Jesus is?"

JESUS: MASTER OF THE "Q AND Q"

Jesus was a master of asking questions that made you sit up and think again. Jesus didn't so much run "Q and A" sessions as "Q and Q" sessions. In fact, he almost never gave a straight answer to a straight question. In the New Testament, Jesus asked 183 questions, gave 3 answers, and answered 307 questions with a question in return like a true rabbi.[6] The New Testament is chockablock with Jesus asking things like the following:

- "What do you want me to do for you?" (Mark 10:51).
- "What is written in the law? What do you read there?" (Luke 10:26).
- "Woman, where are they? Has no one condemned you?" (John 8:10).
- "But who do you say that I am?" (Matthew 16:15).
- "Who touched my garments?" (Mark 5:30).

The point of this approach is to allow the natural curiosity of the human person to draw him or her to an encounter with the person of Jesus. It is what we see continually happening in the New Testament. Nobody ever yawns in the presence of Christ. Strangers ask who he is, how he can open the eyes of the blind, and how he can speak with an authority that not only outshines the scribes and Pharisees but also commands the obedience of the wind, waves, and evil spirits. His disciples are, if anything, even more curious about him than the crowds who do not know him.

Jesus welcomes and cultivates that curiosity. In the Gospel of John, we find him constantly making statements that pull his hearers into wondering what he could mean: "Destroy this temple and in three days I will raise it up" (John 2:19); "Unless one is born of water and the Spirit, he can-

---

6 Ibid., p. 54.

not enter the kingdom of God" (John 3:5); "Unless you eat the flesh of the Son of man and drink his blood, you have no life in you" (John 6:53); "Before Abraham was, I am" (John 8:58). Every one of these highly charged sayings was bound to provoke, as a first reaction, intense curiosity. Jesus was able to live with that, even when the curiosity turned, as it sometimes did, to bewilderment or even hostility.

This is a place where we need to follow in our Lord's footsteps. When we live lives that are inexplicable apart from the grace and power of the Gospel, we will often find that curiosity is sparked among people who were formerly hostile to the faith.

> To be a witness does not consist in engaging in propaganda, nor even in stirring people up, but in being a living mystery. It means to live in such a way that one's life would not make sense if God did not exist.[7]

A brilliant young pastoral associate friend is experimenting with question-based seeker groups. These are groups for people of any background who would like to discuss spiritual questions that really matter to them. He does not spend his time giving presentations on Catholic teaching but on preparing and throwing out great questions and the occasional scriptural or magisterial quote and then letting the groups wrestle with the issues themselves. One of his observations:

> We had an absolutely great seeker session last night! The walls are starting to come down, and the real questions emerge. In fact, my "answering" some

---

[7]   Emmanuel Cardinal Suhard, *Priests Among Men* (Chicago: Fides, 1949).

questions can delay the necessary spiritual quest that is emerging. Also, it can communicate the wrong concept about faith, as though being a Catholic were merely a matter of intellectual assent to "ideas."

One powerful way to rouse curiosity is to tell stories. Again, Jesus was masterful in his use of parables and stories. Telling stories of Jesus from the New Testament and stories of your own or someone else's experiences of healing and forgiveness can be very thought provoking.

Curiosity Is Not Seeking

Curiosity is important but still essentially casual and passive. Curiosity involves trust but not openness to change — not yet. And it is certainly not the intense spiritual quest of true seeking. Curiosity is natural. The curious Jews of John 8 "believed in Jesus" in the sense that they saw and heard some remarkable things and so hung around for a while to get a look at Jesus, the latest nine-day wonder. Such curiosity *can* issue in discipleship but need not. (See the end of John 8 to see how curiosity, if it does not blossom into discipleship, can turn against Christ.)

One of the high points of our Making Disciples seminars, after introducing participants to the thresholds, is watching a DVD of Daniel Moore telling the story of his remarkable journey through serious drug addiction to discipleship. Daniel's story is very powerful. He speaks in simple, direct language, and participants always find his testimony very moving.

We divide the video into five sections that correspond with certain developments in Daniel's life. We stop after every section and ask participants to talk about what they think is going on at this point in Daniel's life. What threshold do they think he is at by the end of this segment? This always generates a fascinating discussion, as people naturally hear different things and have different opinions about the spiritual significance of events and actions that Daniel describes.

For all the diversity of responses, one thing happens over and over again. During the first break, there are people who think that Daniel is already an intentional disciple. It is only as his story progresses that they begin to see the enormous gap between where Daniel is at the beginning and where God has taken him by the end. By the fourth break, their understanding of the significance of the major turning points in Daniel's life has totally changed because their understanding of discipleship has changed.

What many participants find hard to grasp at first is the difference between *passively* going with the flow and a truly *active* spiritual quest. Daniel does not resist a friend's suggestion that he go through RCIA (after receiving an emergency baptism because he was in danger of death), and many regard this as an obvious sign of active personal faith. As we led these sessions, however, we slowly came to realize that a significant number of Catholic leaders, even those deeply interested in evangelization, think of faith as essentially passive. By this reckoning, if you show up, and unless you obviously fight or reject the precepts of the Church, you have "faith."

This is another area in which our perception of what "normal" Christianity looks like is shaped by our experience. We have come to accept passivity as "normative" Catholicism because the majority of Catholics are, in fact, spiritually passive. All the statistical indicators suggest that the majority of our "active" members are in early and essentially passive stages of spiritual development, such as trust and curiosity.

It has been our experience that the communal spiritual norm of an average American parish — one that is not influenced by an evangelizing or other special movement — is usually somewhere between trust and curiosity. As we'll see in the following chapters, if this is true in your parish, it has significant implications for all areas of parochial life, especially when a parish starts to intentionally evangelize.

Living Curiously

The Catholic life is to be a "sign of contradiction" in this world. That doesn't mean we are to be nay-saying curmudgeons. Rather, it means we are to live lives of such inexplicable joy, love, faith, and peace (even in trial) that all the normal categories by which nonbelievers try to classify us won't work. We are neither Jew nor Gentile, fish nor fowl, "conservative" nor "liberal," nor any of the other tribes of this world. As Hebrews 13:14 says, "Here we have no lasting city, but we seek the city which is to come."

Living curiously means more than being "nice." It requires that we think and act in Kingdom-oriented and countercultural ways in our daily lives. For instance, forgiving and asking forgiveness of those who have betrayed and abused us are perhaps the most countercultural things we can do — far more difficult and far more radically wonder-evoking than the moral teachings concerning sexuality that the media assume are the most difficult aspects of the Catholic faith.

Likewise, speaking the truth in love, honoring others with our words, living in healthy relationships, caring for the poor, sharing possessions freely, praying for healing and provision, and even simple family prayer times can be startling countercultural witnesses. We have the freedom in Christ to say unexpected and even borderline outrageous things, not to shock but to genuinely "subvert the dominant paradigm" with the prospect that the Kingdom of heaven is here, that the risen and supernatural Lord Jesus Christ is in our midst with power.

A prayerful life that springs from the supernatural power of the Eucharist and the sacraments and issues in the corporal and spiritual works of mercy such as feeding the hungry, caring for the sick, and praying for the living and the dead can be a powerful sign of contradiction that creates the curiosity that calls a soul to Christ. As Pope Benedict has written:

> Testimony to Christ's charity, through works of justice, peace and development, is part and parcel of evangelization, because Jesus Christ, who loves us, is concerned with the whole person.[8]

---

[8]   Pope Benedict XVI, *Caritas in Veritate*, 15.

Helping Catholics Come Home

Parish-based outreaches like Landings and Catholics Returning Home were created to restore the trust of those who have left the Church. They do so through the hospitality and acceptance of a group of practicing Catholics.

Another outreach, the Catholics Come Home (CCH) campaign, has fostered trust and curiosity through television ad campaigns in thirty dioceses between 2008 and 2011. According to the CCH website, the ads have helped "hundreds of thousands to come home" to the Catholic Church. This result is measured in part by a growth in Mass attendance.

However, Mark Gray, director of Catholic polls for the Center for Applied Research in the Apostolate (CARA), has written an extensive review of CCH to date. He notes that within a year, Mass attendance was back to pre-CCH levels. Gray points out that the initial bumps could be due to the fact that CCH campaigns are held during Advent and Lent, times of the year when Catholic attendance always rises significantly:

> I do not doubt the ads bring some "fallen away" Catholics and non-Catholics into parishes. But the data indicate the number of these individuals at this time is still too small to appear in national counts. The CCH materials often speak of "souls saved" by the commercials. For this to be the case the people returning to parishes will have to start showing up and staying.... It has to be more than a "short visit home."[9]

---

[9]   Gray, "Catholics Come Home ... But Just for a Visit?"

In light of the thresholds, we could say that the CCH ads can help reestablish trust and arouse curiosity, but then what? The missing part is our communal parish life. Our parishes haven't suddenly become more hospitable or evangelizing. Restoring the basic elemental bond of trust is a huge step. But the odds are better than 50/50 that those sticking their toes back into the big Catholic ocean are not certain that a personal relationship with God is even possible. Unless what drew them away and sent them seeking in the first place is addressed, chances are our returnees will just be making short visits home.

Most initiatives aimed at lapsed Catholics don't address the question of discipleship. Their impact could be multiplied many times if we understood these outreaches in light of the overall journey that twenty-first-century people typically make. CCH and other returning Catholic outreaches won't have the impact we desire as long as we presume that luring Catholics to cross the threshold again and restoring trust is all that needs to happen. We won't have the impact we desire until intentional discipleship has become our communal norm.

CHAPTER 7

The Third Threshold: Openness

"I believe; help my unbelief!"

MARK 9:24

Shortly after we began working with the thresholds, I received an e-mail from a man in Australia whom I will call "Thomas." Thomas wanted to talk to me about a surprising development in his relationship with a work colleague. "Gareth" and Thomas had worked together for thirty years. Gareth was a lifelong, militant, scientific atheist who had always heaped scorn on Thomas's deep Catholic faith. But six months earlier Gareth's wife had died, and suddenly Gareth turned up on Thomas's doorstep, wanting to talk about God. Somehow, over the years of working together, a bridge of trust had been built, and in this moment of vulnerability Gareth turned to Thomas.

Grief didn't make Gareth any easier to deal with. He would borrow books like St. Thérèse's *Story of a Soul*, and a week later he'd throw the book down on Thomas's table, declare it to be rubbish — and then borrow three more books. It required tremendous patience and prayer on Thomas's part to put up with Gareth's tantrums, and occasionally I'd get an intensely frustrated e-mail from Thomas — it all seemed so pointless. Gareth would rant endlessly about the stupidity of the very idea of God and attack Thomas's beliefs, and yet very slowly, despite his kicking and screaming,

Gareth was changing. After several years, he acknowledged that he believed that God existed. But as for an organized religion like Catholicism — hah!

Then came the day when Gareth asked Thomas if he could go to an RCIA session with him. I got the news about Gareth's decision to attend RCIA a few days before I had to speak to a large archdiocesan gathering of RCIA leaders on the thresholds. When I covered the threshold of openness, I told the story of Thomas and Gareth. Just out of curiosity, I asked the crowd how they'd feel about having a Gareth in their RCIA program. The consternation on their faces said it all. The prospect of a Gareth loose in a typical RCIA was enough to make the toughest catechist quail!

It was not exactly a surprise when Gareth decided after a single session that RCIA wasn't for him. He came to the same conclusion on his second experiment with RCIA. Perhaps the third time will be the charm. (Who am I to criticize? I am a survivor of three RCIAs and graduate of none.) But Gareth is still dropping by Thomas's house, and the talk almost always turns to Christianity and faith.

Whenever I think of the threshold of openness, I think of Gareth. Curiosity is a God-given part of being human that is naturally ordered to ultimate fulfillment in God. Under the influence of grace, it is intended to lead on to the next threshold: openness. But moving into that threshold is one of the most difficult journeys for twenty-first-century people to make because it demands that we declare ourselves open to the possibility of personal and spiritual change. Openness is the premier example of a decision point that can feel dramatically different for outsiders than for insiders. The one on the verge of openness can feel as if he or she is teetering on the edge of an abyss, while the lifelong Catholic wonders what all the fuss is about.

Despite all his protests, Gareth has actually undergone significant spiritual change and is haunting the frontier of openness. Whether or not he will be able to make the final plunge into openness is the question about which Thomas and I have been praying for years.

Moving from curiosity to openness is one of the hardest transitions to make because it involves, as earlier thresholds do not, making the choice to lower such defenses as cynicism and antagonism, and acknowledge to God (if he is really there and listening) and to oneself that you are open to change. It can feel dangerous, crazy, frightening, and out of control. There are many internal and external pressures, fears, and blocks that must be overcome to reach openness. Because of this, many who are curious never make this transition.

Pope Benedict XVI touched upon this dynamic beautifully in his inaugural homily:

> If we let Christ enter fully into our lives, if we open ourselves totally to him, are we not afraid that He might take something away from us? Are we not perhaps afraid to give up something significant, something unique, something that makes life so beautiful? Do we not then risk ending up diminished and deprived of our freedom?[1]

---

[1] Pope Benedict XVI, *Inaugural Homily*, April 24, 2005 (online at http://www.vatican.va/holy_father/benedict_xvi/homilies/documents/hf_ben-xvi_hom_20050424_inizio-pontificato_en.html, as of May 8, 2012).

Openness to change is often triggered by a major life event. It can be the vulnerability that comes with unemployment or switching careers. It can be some new relationship such as falling in love, marriage, or having children (with all the reassessment of previous assumptions these can bring). It can also be the wounding or death of a relationship or the death of a spouse. It can be a grave illness, a tragedy, or some other kind of loss. It can be a major turning point such as returning to the marketplace after your children are in school, graduation, or retirement. It can be a spiritual reawakening sparked by contemplating the intricate beauty of a child's ear (as it was for former communist Whittaker Chambers) or by a conversation with friends (as it was for C. S. Lewis during a famous walk with J. R. R. Tolkien and Hugo Dyson).

For every person who negotiates the journey to openness without struggle, there are ten for whom it is very difficult. Many, like Gareth, go back and forth between wanting change and being opposed to change. As people approach the threshold of openness, some "try on" what it would be like to change. They give God a trial run, so to speak. As they do so, we need to stifle the impulse to say, "You just have to believe." We must resist the urge to pressure them beyond what they are prepared to do right then. If your friend doesn't yet believe in a personal God or doesn't think a relationship with God is possible, he won't be able to cross into openness. The fundamental issues must be dealt with first.

Since the journey to openness may well be a slow process, patience is vital. We need to remember that our friend's surface questions about large cosmic issues may well hide deeper personal questions that drive the search and yet make it difficult to move forward. Serious, enduring intercession is especially critical when someone is on the verge of openness. That is because God is not the only one at work in this process. Many influences — the person's wounded nature, family dynamics, unhealthy or hostile friends, as well as the culture, the enemy, and the world — all conspire to block a move into openness. And our care for the person must be genuine. No matter what our friend decides, he or she needs to know that we truly are friends.

Don't Jump the Gun

As I have noted before, Catholics often confuse early thresholds like trust with active personal faith, or curiosity with serious seeking. We can also confuse an initial openness to change with intentional discipleship. The implications of this confusion became clearer to Father Mike and me a few years ago when an Iowa couple consulted with us about their evangelization efforts.

"Samantha" had been leading a popular local evangelizing parish retreat for years. Her husband, "George," had gone on one of the weekends and experienced a dramatic conversion. George came out of the retreat a passionate disciple and was now heavily involved in RCIA and the retreats. After learning about the thresholds, Samantha and George recognized something was happening at the weekends that they had not grasped before.

They realized that many parishioners' lives were genuinely changed by the retreats — but also that most left the events at the threshold of openness rather than as full-fledged disciples. Parishioners had moved from trust or curiosity into openness in the course of a few days, so their experience was intense and vivid. In addition, just by acknowledging their openness to personal change, they had already moved beyond the communal spiritual norm. Because what the retreatants experienced was so powerful and because few had a vivid sense of what intentional discipleship looked like, it had never occurred to anyone that there was more to the journey.

Since many Catholics presume that spiritual change naturally happens at a glacial pace, to see someone go through rapid change is dramatic indeed. What more could you ask? The expectation in this couple's parish was that you went through the retreat to get "excited" about your faith, and then you would get busy expressing that faith by serving in the parish. As a result, there was no provision for follow-up, much less any concerted effort to help retreat alumni continue on to intentional discipleship.

Catholics who move into a stage of spiritual development that is beyond their particular community's experience may quickly discover that their family, friends, and fellow parishioners are uncomfortable with this new development. What we are discovering is that some are so distressed by the lack of support in their parish that they actually leave to find a community that understands what has happened to them. "Rachel," who works in a large archdiocese, recently had six different people, all unrelated, approach her over the course of a single month and tell her, "I am on the verge of leaving the Church for a Protestant church, because I don't know anyone in the parish that I can talk to about what is happening to me spiritually." Word had gone around the parish that you could talk to Rachel about spiritual issues and a relationship with God. Happily, she was able to convince four out of the six to stay. She connected them with people and groups in the parish who could support them in their journey.

We need to recognize the presence of a *hidden hemorrhage fueled by spiritual growth* in our parishes. Numerous Catholics are experiencing spiritual longings but may have little or no language for what they seek. They sense there has to be more to faith than what they have encountered so far. In terms of thresholds, these people range from the later stages of curiosity through openness and early seeking. Their spiritual antennae are up, and they are quietly looking for people who might know, for clues, for guidance. But they are often invisible to the rest of us. If they hesitantly come to talk to parish staff or leaders, the response is most often to try to connect them with some parish or diocesan activity.

These seekers are part of the group that told Pew Researchers that they left the Catholic Church because their "spiritual needs weren't being met." Many of them eventually enter the Protestant world. (Nine percent of all Protestants and 11 percent of all evangelicals were raised Catholic.) These people are motivated by a different kind of loss: a loss of spiritual hope that eventually turns into a loss of trust. Rebuilding or strengthening the trust of those who have left or are considering leaving because they long for more than they see around them requires that we be able to give them hope that their spiritual hungers will be met abundantly in and through the Catholic Church. For most, that will have to happen at the parish level.

What we are beginning to see is that when the topic of discipleship and personal relationship with God is talked about openly in the parish, these hidden seekers start emerging out of the shadows. If they think there is a possibility that someone will understand, many will seek help within the Church before they leave. And if they find that help, most don't leave. If they can't find help in their own parish, they will often turn to another parish that is overtly focusing on discipleship. Such parishes find that spiritual seekers and disciples come to them. Talk about low-hanging fruit! These people are in our midst. They are already baptized, already Catholic. All we need to do is recognize, honor, nourish, and support the work of the Holy Spirit in their hearts, and we will gain many radiant new disciples.

FOSTERING OPENNESS

On the verge of openness, it can be helpful to challenge your friend appropriately to take the next step. Jesus did this constantly, sometimes resulting in someone's renouncing his life to follow him (as with the apostles) and sometimes resulting in a potential disciple going away sad (as with the rich young man). Obviously, a deep trust between the two of you must already be in place. Here are a few suggestions:

- **Practice nonjudgmental truthfulness.** Talk about your own struggles of faith, how you look to God to enable you to change, and your experience of his helping you change.
- **Ask thought-provoking questions.** Often people on the edge of openness can be helped with well-timed

questions that raise the issue of personal change: "What do you do when life gets hard?" or "Where is God in all this for you?"

- **Help them connect the dots.** In our discernment work, we spend a great deal of time helping Catholics recognize ways that they are already being used by God that have escaped their notice. The same dynamic is helpful when accompanying someone on the verge of openness. *Using their own words as much as possible*, remind them how God has been at work in their lives to this point. It can help them see that God is pursuing them in love and doing all he can to get their attention.

- **Encourage them to ask God for a sign.** Yes, this is daring, but do we believe that God is initiating a relationship with them or not?

- **Ask them if you can pray for them to be open to God.** If they give you permission, consider praying for this in front of them in your own words. Keep it as simple as possible. I know this can be anxiety producing for many Catholics, but there is tremendous power for some in hearing someone else putting such a prayer into words.

- **Ask them if they would be willing to pray themselves and acknowledge their openness to God.** Of course, this is the ultimate goal. But when it happens, it can seem simple and nondramatic.

The Catholic tradition holds that grace perfects nature (since God is the author of both). So it is important to take advantage of whatever aspects of human culture will help the potential disciple. One advantage we can capitalize on is the fact that, in our culture, openness is a *good* thing. This cultural imperative to remain open to new ideas and experiences can help immensely in encouraging the person growing toward discipleship to grasp the fact that Jesus transforms lives, and that openness to change and growth will ultimately issue in their happiness and blessing.

GOD WITH US

One very simple and nonthreatening way to help foster trust, curiosity, and openness is Eucharistic Adoration. What if we stop thinking of Adoration as primarily a devotion for the already devout and consider it also as a form of evangelization particularly suited to the postmodern mind-set? It is, in fact, an ideal form of devotion for the nondevout.

Adoration appeals to postmoderns because it is experiential, mysterious, and accessible to everyone: the non-baptized, the non-Catholic, the unchurched, the lapsed, the badly catechized, the wounded, the skeptical, the seeking, the prodigal, and those who aren't sure that a relationship with God is even possible. An acquaintance of mine aptly describes it as "Spiritual Radiation Therapy" because it places the soul in the direct presence of Jesus Christ in the trust that he will act if we leave the door open the merest crack. All it requires is the ability to sit down.

This is how one parish leader describes using Adoration to draw the baptized into a deeper relationship with Christ:

> One of the biggest things our community lacked was an experience of the supernatural dimension of the Christian life. It just wasn't on our radar.

They had "unintentional" encounters in the liturgy but never something that they felt or experienced as having an impact. Eucharistic Adoration with teens and adults has been a powerful experience of the presence of Christ. Eucharistic Adoration gives them an experience of encountering God.

I have heard many stories of conversions triggered by "accidental" exposure to the Blessed Sacrament. I myself am Catholic today because I encountered the Blessed Sacrament when I was a completely clueless college student. I had gone through a major conversion experience the year before and was looking for a place to pray during the day. Protestant churches were closed, but a large Gothic Catholic church nearby was open during the day, although I had no idea why. I walked into Blessed Sacrament Church (!) and *felt* a powerful presence of God that I had never felt before. In an instant, that experience of God's presence leapt over the anti-Catholicism of my fundamentalist childhood, and a most unexpected bridge of trust was suddenly in place.

It was that experience of God's presence that kept me coming back to Catholic churches to pray. I would walk into lovely Protestant churches and think, "It's beautiful but empty." That Presence-for-which-I-had-no-explanation wasn't there. And so I came to regard Blessed Sacrament as my personal prayer place. Nevertheless, my evangelical identity was still firmly in place, and I wasn't open to changing.

Then, one day as I prayed inside Blessed Sacrament, I stopped in front of a statue of what was clearly a young woman. A sign told me that her name was Catherine of Siena. I didn't know anything about Catherine, but I knew that she must be a saint and that Catholics believed that you could ask saints to pray for you.

On impulse I did. "Kate," I said, "you understand what it is like to be a young woman. They say that I can ask you to pray for me. I want so much to find the purpose for which God has created me. I need to know what I am supposed to do. If you can, please pray that I find it." And then, for reasons I still don't understand, I suddenly lifted my head and directed my next prayer to the ceiling. "And, God, if there's anything to this Catholic thing, I'm open."

The next moment I mentally dismissed the whole idea as possibly the wildest, stupidest thing I had ever done. But I didn't take it back. I didn't grasp the full significance of that moment until I discovered the thresholds many years later. I had acknowledged to myself and to God that I was *open* to personal change. I had crossed, without knowing it, into a new spiritual world.

As a human heart opens to Jesus Christ, it becomes increasingly difficult to remain neutral. The person growing closer to discipleship must cross the next great frontier, from being open to change as a mere possibility to engaging in an active spiritual quest. He or she must cross into the threshold of spiritual seeking.

CHAPTER 8

Thresholds of Conversion: Seeking and Intentional Discipleship

For every man the beginning of life is the moment when Christ was immolated for him. But Christ is immolated for him at the moment he acknowledges grace and becomes conscious of the life obtained for him by means of that immolation.

AN ANCIENT EASTER HOMILY[1]

When Corinne Lopez, director of faith formation at the St. Thomas More Newman Center at the University of Oregon, and her colleague Doug returned from a Making Disciples seminar in October 2007, they knew things had to change. "Although RCIA was already underway when we got back, Doug and I went through our old RCIA outlines and basically threw almost everything out," Corinne told me. "We began asking ourselves, 'Where do we want people to be spiritually when they are baptized or making a profession of faith?'"

---

[1] *Easter Homilies of the year 387* (SCh 36, p. 59ff).

They decided that they needed to change their inquiry process to make it clear that the purpose of RCIA is to help people become conscious, intentional followers of Jesus. The team concentrated on keeping the focus on Jesus. "There was a total openness to seeing how Jesus is the center of all we do as Catholics," Corinne said. "Inquiry wasn't so much about Church history but about Jesus as Lord, Savior, God. We let them know, your Catholic faith will lead you to follow Christ, and if you're following Christ, you'll want to be Catholic." With a greater focus on Christ and the call to conversion, Corinne and her team noticed that the catechumens and candidates were noticeably hungry for solid catechesis. They continued to ask great questions as the team introduced the sacraments and the Church's tradition and social teaching after the Rite of Acceptance at the beginning of Lent.

Father Raniero Cantalamessa detailed this "Jesus first" approach to inquiry before Pope Benedict and the papal household on the last Sunday of Advent 2011:

> So now, if we want to evangelize a secularized world, there is a choice to make. Where do we begin? ... The immense wealth of doctrine and institutions can become a handicap if we are trying to present all of that to a person who has lost all contact with the Church and no longer knows who Jesus is.
>
> Instead, it is necessary to help this person establish a relationship with Jesus. We need to do what Peter did on the day of Pentecost, when 3,000 people were present: to speak about Jesus whom we have crucified and whom God has raised and to bring

that person to the point that he or she, cut to the heart, asks, "Brethren, what shall we do?" (Acts 2:37). We will respond as Peter does, "Repent, and be baptized every one of you" (Acts 2:38) if you have not been baptized, or if you have already been baptized, go to confession.

Those who respond to the proclamation will join themselves — today as in that day — to the community of believers. They will listen to the teaching of the apostles and will partake in the breaking of the bread. Depending on each person's calling and response, little by little they will be able to make the immense heritage arising from the kerygma their own. Jesus is not accepted on the word of the Church, but the Church is accepted on the word of Jesus.[2]

Our primary task when someone has reached the threshold of seeking is to help him or her focus on the person of Jesus and the central challenges of the kerygma, leaving other doctrinal issues for later. If the person is going through RCIA, the catechumenate and mystagogia will afford time for covering these issues and will be vastly more fruitful for those who are disciples.

Whenever we talk about focusing on Jesus, a common concern is that we are talking about a "me and Jesus" mindset, but this is not at all the case. In an RCIA setting or in

---

[2] "Father [Raniero] Cantalamessa's 4th Advent Sermon: 'The Current Wave of Evangelization,'" Zenit, December 23, 2011 (online at www .zenit.org/article-34044?l=english, as of May 8, 2012).

parish-based retreats or other evangelizing experiences, it is ultimately the Church who is proposing Jesus Christ, her Lord and the living heart of all that she believes and holds dear, to seekers. If we did this consistently, we wouldn't have the millions of Catholics in Protestant congregations telling people that they left because they hadn't encountered Christ in a living way as a Catholic. "Me and Jesus" would cease to be an issue if Catholics routinely encountered Jesus Christ in a life-changing way *in the context of their own parishes.*

Nor would we have the problem of huge numbers of RCIA alumni leaving the Church within a year of being received. This was brought home to me in 2000 when Father Michael Sweeney and I did presentations in Rome on the theology behind the Called & Gifted discernment process. We spent over an hour talking about our work with a particular cardinal in his office. At one point, he turned to me and asked, "What percentage of American adults received through RCIA have left the practice of the faith within the first year?"

I wasn't sure but knew the numbers weren't good. So I hazarded a guess: "Fifty percent?"

The cardinal shook his head. "Oh no," he said. "It is closer to 70 percent."

While there is no solid national research on the exact number of neophytes who abandon the practice of the faith within the first year, everyone I've talked with who is involved in catechumenal ministry is aware of and concerned about this reality. When we focus on making disciples in the context of RCIA, the hemorrhage slows to a trickle.

Corinne certainly was concerned that many of her "alumni" would vanish, but as she puts it, "the proof is in the pudding." That first Easter four adults were baptized, while four others made a profession of faith. Through conversations and observing their behavior, Corinne and Doug knew that all eight were either intentional disciples or seeking. Corinne told me: "I thought one of the guys was still seeking, but during his confirmation at the Vigil, he almost keeled over. His sponsor had to hold him. Since then he's cut a Christian-rap CD. He's on fire with faith and is just exciting to be around. He knows and loves Jesus and Mary!"

About thirty-two men and women have entered the Church through RCIA at the Newman Center over the past four years. Most were disciples by the time they finished mystagogia. The RCIA team focuses on helping the neophytes connect with the Church during mystagogia. Several mystagogia classes didn't want to stop even during the summer! Corinne has kept in touch with her neophytes via e-mail, and almost all are active Catholics today. Several have brought other people into RCIA in following years. Four of her RCIA alumni now work for the Church; three as youth ministers.

HEADING INTO "THE ZONE"

We have found it useful to think of the two thresholds of seeking and intentional discipleship as a whole, as well as considering them as two separate stages. What both thresholds have in common is that they are *active* rather than essentially passive like the earlier thresholds of trust, curiosity, and openness. That's why we sometimes talk of seeking and intentional discipleship together as "The Zone."

"The Zone" is the place of active wrestling with and serious contemplation of the following of Christ. When an individual crosses the line into active seeking, things really start to change. When large numbers of parishioners are actively seeking or are disciples, the spiritual atmosphere in the parish heats up dramatically.

Seeking: "Dating with a Purpose"

From the outside, being open can look like seeking. And some people assume that just being "open to the universe" — that is, *not* being closed — is the same as actively seeking. But it isn't.

Being "open" is a fashionable twenty-first-century stance, especially in places like Seattle. For instance, I once saw an eye-catching ad in an alternative Seattle newspaper. For a paltry sum, you could participate in a session with a Vashon Island guru who was, he assured you, receiving the "incoming patterns of the universe." Many postmoderns are very comfortable with the idea of being "open" as long as there is no expectation that they will have to reach a conclusion.

But that sort of openness is light years away from the inner experience of spiritual seeking. To enter into the threshold of seeking requires a certainty that a personal relationship with God is *possible*, because that is, after all, what one is exploring. Seeking is like "dating with a purpose" but not yet marriage. In both these relationships, the questions being asked are very analogous: Is this person the One? Should I give my life to this One?

Marriage is precisely the image that Scripture uses again and again to describe the relationship between God and Israel, Christ and the Church, and the Holy Spirit and the soul. People in the grip of spiritual seeking are no longer speculating about interesting questions with no stake in the outcome. On the contrary, they are now wrestling with a life decision that really matters. They *want*, they *need*, to come to a conclusion. Seeking feels like a quest.

Seekers Seek Jesus

The seeker seeks Jesus Christ and not just God in a general sense or as the "divine," an "impersonal force," or a "Higher Power." Seeking is centered on the possibility of committing oneself to follow Jesus of Nazareth as his disciple. At the same time, seeking is not yet intentional discipleship. You are only seriously *thinking* about dropping your nets and following Jesus into the unknown. Your nets are still very much in your own hands. However, seekers do begin to count the cost as Jesus commanded we do:

> Now great multitudes accompanied him; and he turned and said to them, "If any one comes to me and does not hate his own father and mother and wife and children and brothers and sisters, yes, and even his own life, he cannot be my disciple. Whoever does not bear his own cross and come after me, cannot be my disciple. For which of you, desiring to build a tower, does not first sit down and count the cost, whether he has enough to complete it?" (Luke 14:25–28)

Seekers realize that following Christ has personal implications: it will make real demands on their priorities, time, money, relationships, and all other areas of life. They grasp the fact that discipleship is not just "fire insurance," nor is it mere "mental assent" to a few religious ideas or values.

By the time a spiritual traveler has crossed into seeking, he or she feels comfortable spending a lot of time with Christians. While the inquiry period of RCIA is ideally suited to people in the thresholds of trust, curiosity, and openness, the seeker threshold is the perfect time to enter the formal catechumenate. Initiatory catechesis is incredibly fruitful for seekers, because they are urgently asking the questions that catechesis is intended to answer. It is as a seeker that many begin to pray seriously, become aware of personal sin, and feel the need for personal repentance.

As we move through the thresholds, our knowledge of Jesus and our openness to him should be steadily increasing. Catholics on the way to discipleship can and should be exposed to parts of the Great Story of Jesus (the kerygma) from the threshold of curiosity on. They will need to understand the whole by the time they make a decision whether or not to "drop their nets."

MOVING FROM OPENNESS TO SEEKING

We may sometimes need to challenge a person to continue the journey from openness to seeking. Here it is helpful to remember Jesus' words, "My teaching is not mine, but his who sent me; if any man's will is to do his will, he shall know whether the teaching is from God or whether I am speaking on my own authority" (John 7:16–17).

We can often help those on the frontier of seeking by inviting them to experiment with the corporal and spiritual works of mercy. Rooted in the parable of the sheep and the goats that Jesus told in Matthew 25:31–46, as well as in the rest of the Jewish and Christian moral tradition, the works of mercy call us to address both the physical and spiritual needs of the human person in a hands-on way.[3]

The threshold of seeking is also an excellent time to help them explore the vast diversity of prayer within the Catholic tradition. Different people will respond to different kinds of prayer. If the Rosary does not scratch where a person itches, perhaps the Liturgy of the Hours, *lectio divina*, Eucharistic Adoration, or praise and worship does. Naturally, encourage them to attend Mass, Adoration, prayer and fellowship groups. Better still, invite them to come with you. Introduce them to other disciples so that they can experience the beginnings of Christian community. It can be very powerful for seekers to hear the journeys of new disciples.

It is both challenging and intimidating to realize that, as evangelizers, we need to model what it means to seek after Christ and share how that is going — both the ups and downs. I certainly feel anxious at the thought of exposing some of the reality of my own relationship with God to someone else. But seekers need to see what life is like for an authentic disciple of Jesus whose struggles are real — and whose victories are therefore believable. It is far more important that your relationship with Jesus exists and is real than that it conform to some imaginary template of Catholic perfection. Think about how you could share your

---

[3]   For an excellent introduction to the corporal and spiritual works of mercy, see Mark P. Shea's *The Work of Mercy: Being the Hands and Heart of Christ* (Cincinnati, OH: Servant, 2012).

own experience of prayer with seekers. Offer to pray with your seeking friends. Share how the sacraments, the Mass, and the life of the Church have nourished your relationship with Jesus.

SIN MATTERS

We need to help seekers confront the issues of relativism, personal sin, and "Lordship" — all three of which are rooted in some of the most profound difficulties postmoderns have with the Catholic tradition, since all of them evoke the fear of the loss of personal autonomy. According to Scot McKnight, professor of biblical and theological studies at North Park University, a sense of personal sin usually comes late in the journey, especially for young adults (which he calls iGens or emerging adults):

> Contemporary culture does not provide the average iGen with a profound grasp of what is right and wrong apart from the conviction that assaulting the self is clearly wrong.... Because of trends like the self-esteem movement and the impact of relativism, he concludes that iGens are pre-moral. Mann suggests that they do not feel guilt as much as they feel shame for not achieving what they are designed to accomplish.[4]

But God always provides a way to speak to the heart that is looking for him. Interestingly, focusing on Jesus and

---

[4] McKnight, "The Gospel for iGens."

his proclamation of the Kingdom of God can ultimately lead postmodern young adults to a sense of personal sin:

> Anyone who vividly sketches a community marked by justice, love, peace, and holiness has a message iGens want to hear. The self hidden behind the castle wall is now interested. And I have found that the self-in-a-castle feels shame about systemic sin, and their sensitivity to things like AIDS, poverty, and racism leads inevitably to recognizing the sin in each person. At some point in this movement to the castle door, the iGen will realize that systemic sin is linked to personal sin. Suddenly he or she feels accountable to God.[5]

We can help our friend see that the Catholic tradition honors freedom but teaches that freedom is ordered toward virtue and that its misuse will guarantee the loss of freedom.

Finally, help seekers see what they have to offer us. Don't forget that they are, in a real sense, peers and companions on a common journey. Treat them accordingly, and be open to the fact that they can often meet a need in your life.

INTENTIONAL DISCIPLESHIP

Once our friend has passed through the thresholds of pre-discipleship, she will come to the point where a final decision whether or not to follow Jesus is required of her. You cannot seek forever. The disciples on the Emmaus road ex-

---

[5] Ibid.

pressed it as "Did not our hearts burn within us …?" (Luke 24:32). We might say, "I can't *not* do this!" The point is that a human being reaches the moment where — with complete freedom — she chooses to sell all she has to purchase the Pearl of Great Price and become a follower of Christ (see Matthew 13:45–46).

This is as far from a passive act as a person can get. It requires a searching and deliberate act of the will. That is why the prior journey through the thresholds is so vital. Everything has prepared us for and led us to this moment of decision. The convert is arriving at the point where he is willing to do what Simon Peter, James, and John did:

> [Jesus] said to Simon, "Put out into the deep and let down your nets for a catch." And Simon answered, "Master, we toiled all night and took nothing! But at your word I will let down the nets." And when they had done this, they enclosed a great shoal of fish; and as their nets were breaking, they beckoned to their partners in the other boat to come and help them. And they came and filled both the boats, so that they began to sink. But when Simon Peter saw it, he fell down at Jesus' knees, saying, "Depart from me, for I am a sinful man, O Lord." For he was astonished, and all that were with him, at the catch of fish which they had taken; and so also were James and John, sons of Zebedee, who were partners with Simon. And Jesus said to Simon, "Do not be afraid; henceforth you will be catching men." And when they had brought their boats to land, they left everything and followed him. (Luke 5:4–11)

Dropping your nets and taking the first steps into the world of intentional discipleship is, then, a supremely active choice. Catholic friends, family, and the parish community play a critical role in helping individuals, whether already baptized or not, make this life-changing decision. At this point, it is usually appropriate to ask those who are on the verge of intentional discipleship whether they are ready to make a commitment. This is not "judging" the seeker. This is more like acting as an ambassador from Christ the Bridegroom who is proposing marriage to his bride. A real choice, an adult decision, is required. The right and the power to make that decision are part of human dignity.

Of course, it is possible that those on the brink of intentional discipleship may say no. That is not the end of the world. If someone says no, the first and most obvious thing to do is ask, "Why not?" In other words, find out what the blocks are. Then try to address those blocks or help your friend set them aside for now. Some seekers may want to review the steps of their journey to this decision point.

There is a common question that arises in an RCIA setting when the lived journey of conversion does not jibe with our liturgical schedule (as it often does not). Should we encourage someone to "drop their nets" and follow Christ before they have decided to enter the Church? Absolutely! In fact, encouragement of a person's choice to become a disciple fits the Church's understanding of pre-baptismal disposition perfectly and helps prepare the person to make the commitment to Christ's body, the Church. This is where the value of a year-round RCIA and inquiry becomes obvious. They enable the team to respond to the work of the Holy Spirit in each individual rather than letting the urgency of an impending liturgical season force a premature decision.

Finally, I think it cannot be emphasized strongly enough that spiritual warfare often becomes very intense on the verge of discipleship (as it does on the verge of openness). The same opposition manifests itself as a human being contemplates this choice, which has so many eternal and temporal implications. Tremendous obstacles can suddenly appear. Because of this, sustained intercessory prayer for those making their decisions is crucial.

The story of a remarkable young woman who entered the Church at a Newman Center on the East Coast shows how intense the opposition can be. "Jenn" was an unbaptized young woman who had been raised by atheist parents. She was attracted to the faith originally by a high school friend who was an intentional disciple. Jenn asked lots of questions her freshman year. By her sophomore year, she hungered for the Eucharist. That's when Jenn entered RCIA and even brought a friend.

Jenn's parents were deeply opposed and threatened to cut her off. Nevertheless, Jenn came faithfully every Wednesday to RCIA and Mass. Her mother showed up one Wednesday, pulled her daughter out of the church, and yelled at her, "You are going to go to hell!" Despite everything, Jenn persisted and was baptized at Easter. She had to move home for two weeks after this, and her mom destroyed all the religious articles she had received. Afterward, Jenn called and said, "I love our Lord Jesus and being Catholic, and those are just things." She never wavered, and as time passed, her parents finally accepted her decision. Jenn's radiant faith has inspired curiosity about the Catholic faith in several people, including her boyfriend.

BECOMING A DISCIPLE
FROM A CHRISTIAN BACKGROUND

We have largely been speaking of converts from non-Christian backgrounds so far in this chapter. Of course, a great many adults also enter the Catholic faith from other Christian backgrounds. (As I noted before, 2.6 percent of American adults — about 6.5 million people — are converts to Catholicism.[6]) Many of these are in various stages of pre-discipleship too. Obviously, merely being baptized in a Christian community of any type does not necessarily result in a commitment to discipleship.

Another friend, who heads an RCIA team in the South, has had fascinating experiences with candidates from mainline Protestant backgrounds:

> Some of those who have had an evangelical background already have a relationship with Jesus and want to go deeper, but a lot of the people from mainline Protestant churches haven't considered the relational aspects of their faith.... What we're going to share with them is the story of Jesus, who really lived. When we do this, so much more of the Catholic faith comes alive.... We'll talk about salvation history, the Incarnation, the relationships Jesus had with the apostles and other people; how others sought him out ... and how Jesus is the center of the life that comes from God the Father.

---

6 John L. Allen, Jr., "In America's religious marketplace, the real Catholic problem is new sales," *National Catholic Reporter*, February 11, 2011 (online at http://ncronline.org/blogs/all-things-catholic/americas-religious-marketplace-real-catholic-problem-new-sales, as of May 8, 2012).

"Charlotte" came from a mainline Christian background. What got her interested in Catholicism was that her son ran with a kid who was Catholic. Her son stayed with his friend's family over Saturday nights and went to Mass with them on Sunday. That impressed her — that their faith was important to them. She went through the RCIA process, and when she started to have a relationship with Jesus she decided to quit her job with Planned Parenthood.

Seekers from Christian backgrounds can sometimes move through the thresholds very quickly once trust is established. Parish-based evangelization processes and retreats can help an already baptized individual move from levels one through three into "The Zone" (serious seeking or intentional discipleship) in a single weekend or retreat. (We'll go into more detail about such retreats in chapter 11.)

The liturgical life of the Church is ideally suited to marking the decision to "drop the net" and follow Jesus, for both individuals and the larger Catholic community. This can take many forms, such as a commemoration of one's baptismal day or first confession. Many evangelization processes and retreats have built-in "markers," such as a renewal of the sacraments of initiation or reaffirmation of baptismal and confirmation promises. Converts who are already baptized and already practicing Catholics should be invited to such celebrations. Nothing fosters a widespread culture of discipleship like seeing new disciples from all backgrounds emerge in the parish.

When a Leader Isn't Yet a Disciple

One practical issue that has come up often of late is that of how to help existing leaders — sometimes highly visible diocesan and parish staff — negotiate their own personal journeys to discipleship. One of our collaborators in the Northwest described her experience this way:

> A lot of the pastoral leaders in our parish have still not fully grasped what discipleship is. I invited our pastoral administrator and other staff to Making Disciples and some came. Two of our team went home stunned because they realized for the first time that they hadn't yet made the journey to discipleship.
>
> Our administrator had a huge door open up for her, but when you are involved in pastoral ministry, you are always the leader and you can't really enter into the community with your own personal spiritual and emotional needs. So she doesn't have a place to go with her needs. She lived in our community as a child so everyone knows her. There are only three parishes in our city, and everyone knows her.
>
> Then there is "George": He had this profound experience and is on fire. He didn't know where to go and got involved in everything inside the parish and outside. He had lots of questions regarding discernment and tension in his marriage because of his conversion. But he couldn't find help for the challenges of being a new disciple. I tried to help

him as best I could and meet with him regularly, but I can only do so much. But he has not been able to find anyone else to go to locally who understands his experience of being a disciple.

Those in decision-making roles, who are not yet disciples, don't have a place to go that is safe so that they can get their spiritual needs met. Many come to me privately and share some very profound things. It is tricky for me since it is a double role. I work with them and am their spiritual director/confidant, too.

As leaders, we need to think through, in advance, how to help *all* in our parish who are not yet disciples to negotiate that journey. The issues at stake are extraordinarily high for individuals, for the Christian community, for the Church, and for the world.

CHAPTER 9

Break the Silence

"Now after a long time the master of those servants came and settled accounts with them. And he who had received the five talents came forward, bringing five talents more, saying, 'Master, you delivered to me five talents; here I have made five talents more.' His master said to him, 'Well done, good and faithful servant; you have been faithful over a little, I will set you over much; enter into the joy of your master.'"

MATTHEW 25:19–21

When we asked hundreds of diocesan and parish leaders from sixty dioceses throughout the English-speaking world, "What percent of your parishioners, would you estimate, are intentional disciples?" the consistent answer was "Five percent." How can we change this?

While *we* cannot make anyone "drop their nets" any more than a gardener can make a seed germinate, we can intentionally and intelligently work to create an environment that is conducive to the growth of personal faith and discipleship. We can intentionally shape the atmosphere, experiences, structures, and spiritual culture of our parish life so that it fosters the journey that Jesus Christ asks all of us to make: following him.

THE DOUBLE-IN-FIVE CHALLENGE

One of the first questions to ask is what percentage of *your* parishioners would you estimate are intentional disciples? Regardless of the number that you come up with, *what if your parish leadership committed to doubling the percentage of intentional disciples in your parish over the next five years?"* That is the "double-in-five" challenge. If roughly 2 percent of your parishioners are intentional disciples today, why not shoot for 4 percent five years from now? If you think that roughly 5 percent are disciples right now, what could you do to help raise that percentage to 10 percent? All over the country, we are seeing the transforming impact of setting discipleship goals. Even if you don't make your numeric "goal," you still win because you, your leadership, your parish culture, and the lives of some new disciples will have all been changed.

When Father Ed Pelrine became pastor of Queen of the Rosary Parish in Elk Grove, Illinois, in 2007, he estimated that only 2–3 percent of the parishioners were intentional disciples. Four years later, he believes that disciples now make up 7–10 percent of the parish. This is no accident. Father Ed — with his director of faith formation, Keith Strohm, and the parish's evangelization committee — has set some very specific goals:

1. Increase participation in our small faith communities by 25 percent to support discipleship.
2. Help 15 percent of parishioners to become intentional disciples of Jesus by 2014.
3. Help 40 percent of parishioners to start their discernment of charisms by December 2013.

4. Help parishioners at all levels develop an understanding of the reality of vocation in the Christian life and to offer practical assistance in the discipline of vocational discernment by creating a "school" of vocational discernment for all age groups by February 2013.

When I asked Keith what he hoped would ultimately become true of Queen of the Rosary, he said,

> Almost everyone in the parish would be an intentional disciple and discipleship would be front and center. The expectation that when people come, they know that it's about following Christ and being sent out and living as he asks us to live. You would know it if you visited the parish.

In Michigan, Craig Pohl estimated that between 5–7 percent of parishioners in his small parish were intentional disciples when he joined the parish staff in 2009. Two years later, he says that percentage has nearly doubled to 10–12 percent:

> We ushered over 300 people through our evangelization series and now hear things like "My life is forever different. I have encountered Christ." There is no longer a pervading sense of defensiveness toward evangelization. Father James asked how I would assess where we are, and the words that came to mind were, "The iron is hot right now."

FOUR STEPS TO DOUBLING-IN-FIVE

There are any number of ways that one can begin implementing evangelizing goals, so what follows are essentially suggestions. Nor do I mean to imply that these goals are all encompassing. What I will be describing in the next four chapters are simply the early, first issues that usually need to be addressed in a parish that is serious about making disciples. These suggestions are based upon the experience of parish leaders around the country who are setting out to nurture a parochial norm of discipleship in a thoughtful and systemic way.

The four beginning steps are as follows:

1. Break the silence (as discussed in chapters 9 and 10).
    a. Talk openly about the possibility of a relationship with a personal God who loves you. Talk about your relationship with God.
    b. Talk explicitly about following Jesus: Drop the Name!
    c. Do Ask: Ask others about their lived relationship with God.
    d. Do Tell: Tell the "Great Story of Jesus" (Kerygma).
2. Offer multiple, overlapping opportunities for baptized and nonbaptized people to personally encounter Jesus in the midst of his Church (chapter 11).
3. Expect conversion. Plan for conversion (chapter 12).
4. Lay the spiritual foundation through organized, sustained intercessory prayer (chapter 12).

In this and the next chapter, we will explore the first step: break the silence. In earlier sections, I have already touched upon the necessity of *talking* about Jesus and a relationship with God. In the rest of this chapter, I would like to focus upon the art of asking others about their lived relationship with God. Chapter 10 will cover the art of telling the Great Story of Jesus to postmodern people.

BREAK THE SILENCE!

The Catholic norm of silence can manifest in the strangest ways. When pregnant, unbaptized, teenager Sara Silberger first showed up at a local parish with her Catholic boyfriend, the silence was deafening:

> What troubles me is: An unchurched teen shows up, in a small parish in a small town, week after week, clearly interested in the Mass, with a young man who has been active in the parish since he could walk, and no one wants to tell her the Good News. It would have taken next to nothing. No one said, here, read this, tell me what you think. No one asked me to come to any kind of lecture or meeting, no one prayed with us or said they were praying for us. It's not that I think I'm so special. It's just that … what were they doing? Why didn't they think this was important to do?

A pastoral associate friend recently described another form that our silence can take:

> Many of our parishioners who are emerging intentional disciples have not yet integrated their "cul-

tural Catholic" self with this new, lived reality. It is almost as if they are ashamed and afraid that somehow they are not a faithful Catholic because of this conversion they have experienced.

Another friend wrote from the other end of the country and said that in his parish:

> Because of Catholic culture, disciples often hide the "proof" of their discipleship ... their "works" so that no one accuses them of being prideful. I will say that because of cultural forces that put pressure on disciples to do things in secret, this pool of disciples has not necessarily had an impact directly on the life of the community.

Until discipleship and conversion become a normative part of parish life, many Saras will walk in and out of our parishes untouched, and many Catholics who are disciples will continue to feel that they need to hide or minimize their newly awakened personal faith in front of other Catholics. The first thing that must be done is to deliberately and persistently break the code of silence if it is in place. The Catholic norm of silence about a relationship with God, about Jesus Christ and his story, about our own stories of following Christ, and about the need for everyone to decide whether or not he or she will follow as a disciple is stifling the emergence of a culture of discipleship and all that flows from it. One of the most powerful ways to challenge the silence is by making a safe place for others to talk about their own lived relationship with God.

Do Ask: The Threshold Conversation

Three years ago, I was boarding a plane to Burbank, California. There was a man in my assigned aisle seat already, who apologized but explained that he was undergoing cancer treatment and needed to be able to get to the restroom easily. I sat next to him in his assigned seat and then, on an impulse, I said, "If you want to talk about it, I'm available. I worked my way through graduate school on a cancer unit. You won't scare or unnerve me."

"Mark" turned out to be a producer of family films, and he *did* want to talk. Thus began an intense, nonstop, two-and-a-half-hour conversation about mortal illness, suffering, family, and hope. After an hour, I felt a clear prompting of the Holy Spirit: "Ask him *the* question." And so I did. "Where is God in all this for you?" The conversation took off again with even greater energy about God, faith, Christianity, family, life, death, and hope. When Mark left the plane, he gave me his card, and I told him that I would pray for him. Mark died a few months ago, and I still pray for him.

Once a bridge of trust is in place, people can be surprisingly open to what we have termed "threshold conversations." What do we mean by threshold conversation? It is the initial step of *listening* evangelism, that moment when we invite an individual to talk, simply and directly, about his or her lived relationship with God. We listen prayerfully, seeking to learn what the journey has been like and, if possible, what spiritual threshold she or he is at now. If we take the time to first learn where people have been and where they are now, we can much more effectively encourage them on the journey to intentional discipleship.

The high point of every Making Disciples seminar is always the chance to take part in a live threshold conversation. We invite all kinds of people from the surrounding community to tell their story. Everyone is welcome *except* practicing Catholics, because we want to give those who attend the experience of listening to someone whose experience is really different from their own. "Former" Catholics, Protestants, atheists, "nones," Buddhists, members of 12-Step groups, and nonbelieving or nonpracticing family members and friends have all volunteered to come and tell the story of their lived relationship with God. It is almost always a wonderful and revealing experience for both sides. Catholics discover that no one dies or is traumatized by talking about God, and our volunteers are affected in surprising ways. One man crossed into a whole new threshold just through the act of describing his experience of God! Some of our volunteers enjoy it so much that they volunteer again and again.

A threshold conversation is a simple but incredibly powerful evangelizing tool that simultaneously breaks the silence and raises the central issue that underlies all that we are and do as Catholics. You can have a fruitful threshold conversation in as little as ten minutes, although some will go much longer if both parties have the time. Parish life is full of perfect opportunities for threshold conversations: RCIA, returning-Catholics programs, retreats, sacramental and marriage preparation, adult faith formation, spiritual direction, and pastoral counseling. We routinely incorporate short threshold conversations into our gifts-discernment interviews. You can even have these conversations with strangers sitting next to you on a plane or with family, friends, and acquaintances, as long as a solid bridge of trust is in place.

A threshold conversation is a supportive, inviting, open-ended, prayerful act of listening evangelization. In such conversations, we must listen to more than the facts: we need to hear the emotion and meaning behind the story as well. During a threshold conversation, the goal is *not* catechizing or correcting their ideas — no matter how wildly inaccurate their beliefs or perceptions of the faith or the Church might be. It is also critical to remember that *a threshold conversation is not faith sharing*. During this conversation, we focus on *listening* to the other and set aside the need to share our own story. Neither is it counseling or apologetics, and certainly a threshold conversation is never judgmental.

The ABC's of a Threshold Conversation

Threshold conversations are extremely simple. You begin with some variation of the basic question: *Can you describe your relationship with God to this point in your life?* or *Can you tell me the story of your relationship with God so far?* As we have listened to people, we have learned that the resulting conversation almost always goes in one of five basic directions:

1. "I don't believe in God" (atheist) conversation.
2. "I don't know if there is a God" (agnostic) conversation.
3. "I believe in a Higher-Power or Impersonal Force" conversation.

4. "I believe in a personal God but have no relationship with God" conversation.
5. "I believe in a personal God and have a relationship with God" conversation.

Of course, baptized Catholics can and do respond with any of the answers above. In the fifth category — "I believe in and have a relationship with a personal God" — we not only find intentional disciples but also many non-practicing or lapsed Catholics, believing members of non-Christian faiths, and "nones" who think of themselves as having a relationship with God but do not identify with any religious tradition or community. I know a baptized woman from a Jewish background who says that she has a relationship with Jesus but no longer considers herself to be a Christian. She attends a synagogue where the rabbi is an atheist. When I asked her how she nourished her relationship with Christ, she said she attended evangelical Bible studies!

There is often a vast and surprising gap between people's lived relationship with God and any religious "labels" that they may use when talking to others. That is why a cardinal rule of threshold conversations is *"Never accept a 'label' in the place of a story."* Always ask what people mean by whatever religious "label" they use to describe their own beliefs. It doesn't matter if the person calls herself a "practicing Catholic," an atheist, an agnostic, or a Buddhist. Postmodern people can use religious or spiritual terms in very idiosyncratic ways; consequently, standard dictionary definitions are often of little use here. When people describe themselves as "atheist," they may *not* mean that they don't believe in God. When they call themselves "agnostic," they may *not* really mean they aren't sure if God exists.

For example, 55 percent of self-identified "agnostics" told Pew surveyors that they believed in God and 14 percent that they believed in a personal God. Twenty-nine percent don't believe in God at all. Only 16 percent said they "didn't know." Twenty-five percent of "agnostics" pray at least a few times a month, and 37 percent believe in miracles. So if a person self-identifies as an atheist or agnostic, or says he "doesn't believe," that's not the end of the conversation at all. It's just the beginning.

I heard a Protestant pastor tell a fascinating story a few years ago. He had introduced himself to a man who had just recently begun attending the church. The visitor quickly told the pastor that he was an "atheist." The pastor wisely responded, "Really? Tell me about the God you don't believe in. I may not believe in that God either." As the man told his story, it became clear that what he meant by calling himself an "atheist" was that he didn't believe in the God of his sister, who was involved with an extremist fundamentalist group. The pastor was able to say with complete sincerity that he didn't believe in that God either. Then he asked his visitor to talk about the God he *did* believe in. Three months later, the "atheist" was a committed disciple and member of the church.

We can always respond to those who describe themselves as "atheist" by asking questions like these:

- What do you mean by "atheist"?
- Tell me about the God you don't believe in.

- Do you believe in any *other* kind of God or universal spirit?

If the person says yes to that last question, ask, "Can you describe the God you *do* believe in?" and take the conversation in the direction that matches his response. Conversely, if the person says that he doesn't really believe in any other kind of God, there are still fruitful ways to continue the conversation. You can ask:

- Have you ever believed in God? If so, why did you stop?
- Do you ever pray? If so, how? (Yes, some "atheists" pray!)
- What gives meaning to your life?

One important issue to keep in mind throughout is this: *Does this person have a bridge of trust in place and where is it?* If there is no trust in place, you may be the one who has to foster that trust. To find out, consider asking questions like these:

- Have you had any significant exposure to religion or spirituality at some point? Have you ever attended a religious congregation or school?
- Are you close to any religious or spiritual person(s)? Why do you like/trust him or her? What role does God play in his or her life? How do you feel about that?
- Could you ever imagine believing in God? If so, what would that God be like?

In short, our goal in threshold conversations is to listen for what the Church calls the "seeds of the Word"[1] and to "reverently lay bare the seeds of the Word which lie hidden" in our neighbor. We are to trust that "the Spirit is at work in the heart of every person, through the seeds of the Word.... The Spirit, therefore, is at the very source of man's existential and religious questioning."[2] The " 'seeds of the Word' can constitute a true 'preparation for the Gospel.' "[3]

This may be the first time anyone has asked this person a question about his or her relationship with God and really listened. Just asking such a question raises the issue of a lived relationship with God for those who may never have thought about it before or even known that a personal relationship with God is possible. And surprisingly, giving people the chance to say what they really think does not necessarily reinforce their unbelief. When people have the chance to *fully* articulate what they believe — perhaps for the first time — they may become open for the first time to a truly new perspective. Upon reflection, the seeker may not be satisfied with the answer he originally gave.

We need to ask only two basic questions in a threshold conversation. The first one is this: *"What has your relation-*

---

[1]   *Ad Gentes* (Decree on the Missionary Activity of the Church), 11 (online at http://www.vatican.va/archive/hist_councils/ii_vatican_council/documents/vat-ii_decree_19651207_ad-gentes_en.html, as of May 8, 2012).

[2]   Pope John Paul II, *Redemptoris Missio* (On the Permanent Validity of the Church's Missionary Mandate), 28 (online at http://www.vatican.va/holy_father/john_paul_ii/encyclicals/documents/hf_jp-ii_enc_07121990_redemptoris-missio_en.html, as of May 8, 2012).

[3]   Pope Paul VI, *Evangelii Nuntiandi*, 53.

ship with God been like to this point in your life?" And most threshold conversations can conclude with this second question: *"If you could ask God one question that you knew he would answer right away, what would it be?"*

This question is important because the answer is usually a reflection of current questions, struggles, or felt needs that you might be able to address in the future or that some person or resource in the parish might be able to address. For instance, structuring the inquiry part of RCIA around the urgent questions that come out in threshold conversations with inquirers can be a very powerful way to help people move into curiosity, openness, and even seeking.

As they talk, we attentively listen for these points:

1. Do you believe in God?
2. *What kind of God* do you believe in? (Personal or impersonal?)
3. Do you believe in the *possibility* of a relationship with this God?
4. Do you *have a relationship* with this God? What kind of relationship?
5. Are you part of a religious tradition? What tradition? Are you a Christian?
6. Are there bridges of trust in your life regarding Christ, the Church, the faith, or a committed Christian you know?
7. Do you have a relationship with Jesus Christ?
8. What spiritual threshold are you at? Trust? Curiosity? Openness? Seeking? Intentional disciple?
9. If you are not a disciple, how can I help you take the next step on the journey to discipleship?

During the conversation, our minds must work at two levels at once. We must take in what the person is sharing (which we may find very moving or challenging at a personal level), and we must focus on where her story touches upon the pivotal moments in her spiritual journey. People can drop in and out of a *spontaneous* threshold conversation quite naturally in the middle of a longer conversation. Indeed, the threshold part of a longer conversation may only last five or ten minutes. During the threshold portion, answer factual questions briefly, and then ask a question in return that invites the person to share more of his or her story. Let each person begin at the beginning and tell his story in an order that makes sense to him. Ask clarifying questions if you need to. When the other person wants to change the subject, let her do so. Entrust the fruit of the conversation to God.

Of course, in addition to listening to people's personal stories, we need to tell *the story*, the Great Story of Jesus that awakens initial Christian faith and discipleship.

CHAPTER 10

Do Tell:
The Great Story of Jesus

*Christ Jesus ... emptied himself ... and became obedient
unto death, even death on a cross. Therefore God has
highly exalted him..., that at the name of Jesus ... every tongue [should] confess that Jesus Christ is Lord.*

PHILIPPIANS 2:5, 7–11

My friend Mark Shea had an experience that speaks
volumes about the spiritual literacy of twenty-first-
century Americans. He was at work when his coworker's
radio began playing Joan Osborne's "If God Was One of
Us." Mark's coworker looked thoughtful for a moment and
then said, "Wouldn't that be a great idea for a story?"
Mark said, "What?"

She replied, "*Suppose God became a human being.*
Wouldn't that make a great story?"

The woman speaking was a college-educated professional living and working in the heart of one of the great
urban centers of a nation ostensibly filled with Christians.
She was genuinely surprised when Mark explained that her
"story idea" was in fact *the Great Story* that has dominated
Western history for 2,000 years.

We must be clear: The purpose of evangelization is *not* waking up a generic "faith." Evangelizers seek to bring people to an encounter with the person of Jesus of Nazareth, born of the Virgin Mary, crucified under Pontius Pilate, and risen from the dead. Our own personal witness can help illuminate and make living, compelling, and believable aspects of Jesus' story, *but it cannot take the place of Jesus' story*. As Father Cantalamessa preached in front of Pope Benedict and the papal household:

> To re-evangelize the post-Christian world it is indispensable, I believe, to know the path followed by the Apostles to evangelize the pre-Christian world! …
>
> … The preaching, or kerygma, is called the "gospel"; the teaching, or didache, instead is called the "law," or the commandment of Christ that is summarized in charity. These two things, the first — the kerygma, or gospel — is what gives origin to the Church; the second — the law, or the charity that springs from the first — is what draws for the Church an ideal of moral life, which "forms" the faith of the Church. In this connection, the Apostle distinguishes before the Corinthians his work of "father" in the faith from that of the "pedagogues" who came after him. He says: "For it is I, through the Gospel, who has begotten you in Christ Jesus" (1 Corinthians 4:15).
>
> Therefore, *faith as such flowers only in the presence of the kerygma*, or the announcement. "How are they to believe" — writes the Apostle speaking of faith in Christ — "in him of whom they have never

heard? And how are they to hear without a preacher?" Literally, "without someone who proclaims the kerygma" (*choris keryssontos*). And he concludes: "So faith comes from what is heard, and what is heard comes by the preaching of Christ" (Romans 10:17), where by "preaching" the same thing is understood, that is, the "gospel" or kerygma.[1]

If Christian faith flowers only in the presence of the kerygma, what does that mean for our pastoral practice? How is our generation to believe without someone who proclaims the kerygma? We can no longer presume that people around us already know the story. On the contrary, we have to presume that (a) many don't know the basic facts of the Story; (b) a good deal of what they "know" may be wrong; (c) they don't know how the parts of the story fit together to make a whole; and (d) they don't know what the story means for them personally. Nor do they know what it means for their family, friends, neighbors, coworkers, or the world.

To be sure, telling the story requires that we respect the religious and spiritual situation in which each person finds himself. We must be sensitive to the tempo and pace at which people move through the stages of pre-discipleship. We must absolutely respect their consciences and convictions. But we still have a duty to provide opportunities for them to make a real spiritual choice to follow Christ. We must respect their right to hear the Story.[2]

---

[1] "Father Cantalamessa on Christ Yesterday and Today (Part I)," emphasis added.

[2] Pope Paul VI, *Evangelii Nuntiandi*, 80.

THE STORY AND SPIRITUAL DEVELOPMENT

In every individual's life, there are two fundamental dynamics at work: (1) the individual's personal spiritual journey through the thresholds and (2) his or her knowledge of the Great Story of Jesus. An individual can be spiritually far ahead or far behind his or her knowledge of the kerygma, depending on circumstances, openness to the Spirit, and opportunities.

For instance, Daniel Moore, the young meth addict, was in a struggle for his life and *knew* that he was sinful and hurting others. Although Daniel had always regarded himself as Catholic, he was not baptized until he was nineteen, and his knowledge of the kerygma was limited to distorted snippets of evangelical Protestant sayings that he had heard from his friends. Daniel's readiness for personal change far outstripped his knowledge of the Story.

Some know the "facts" of the Story but have not grasped the meaning, because they have not yet broken through to trust, much less openness or seeking. One of my friends who is running a "seeker" group for Catholics witnessed this interaction a few months ago:

> One of the participants really opened up. She is a disciple who has been Catholic her whole life. She encountered Jesus through several evangelical events she has attended. She currently has one foot in the Catholic world and another in the evangelical world. She has little trust in the Catholic Church, as she doesn't understand why most Catholics don't have a relationship with Jesus and she doesn't see

the Church producing individuals who have a relationship with Jesus.

She shared with strong emotion how she wants to know why Catholics can't ever rest in the love of the Lord, secure, knowing they are saved. She said, "If I am going to walk away from the Church, it would be for this reason: that we can't rest in the love of the Lord. It doesn't seem right to me that you always have to worry about whether you are going to be with God or not forever."

What was fascinating is that she thought that most Catholics are worried about their salvation! And yet the other Catholics in the group showed little to no concern about salvation at all! There wasn't any "understanding" of what salvation really is and how that gift is received. There was no mention of Jesus and his passion, death, and resurrection having anything to do with salvation. It was as though simply "knowing" about Jesus was somehow vaguely important, but no one really knew why.

Ultimately, it is the two together — an open heart and a response to the Great Story of Jesus — that enables an individual to declare with faith, "Jesus is Lord." Indeed, the two feed each other: learning about Jesus through his story can motivate people to finish the personal journey, while moving through the thresholds enables us to understand the story of Jesus as a whole and respond to it.

TAILORING THE GREAT STORY TO OUR AUDIENCE

St. Paul spoke of being "all things to all" (1 Corinthians 9:22). The essential basics of the kerygma do not vary, but we have to ask this question: *What parts* of the Story does this individual or this family or this group need to hear *when* and *in what order?* This can vary, depending upon the beginning place, the holes in their knowledge, and their questions and concerns. We need to ask the following:

1. Does our friend know the essential "acts" of the Story?
2. Has he or she connected the dots? Does he or she understand the Story as a whole?
3. Does our friend understand the personal significance of the Story?
4. What is or has been his or her response to the Story?

It is often disconcerting for Catholics to realize that the basic kerygma that awakens Christian faith and leads to the Church is not primarily *about* the Church herself. I have run into numerous Catholics who fear that if we talk about Jesus, Catholics will be lured from the Church by the intoxicating discovery that a relationship with God can be personal as well as communal.

We have to come to terms with the reality that, in the United States, *if we don't evangelize our own, someone else will*: evangelicals, Mormons, or independent Christians. The *Atlas of Global Christianity* estimates that over 314 million "evangelism offers" are received every day in the United States. That's an average of *more than one "offer" per person every day*, and the vast majority are aimed at people who are already baptized.[3] If we don't preach the kerygma in our parishes, people *will* hear it in a modified form outside the Church and may come to the mistaken conclusion that it isn't to be found within the Church. Our practice of *not* telling the Great Story clearly and compellingly *within* our parishes has contributed as much to the "me and Jesus" mind-set as anything else.

What follows is a very brief outline of the essential Great Story of Jesus organized with postmodern sensitivities in mind. People do *not* have to hear the different "Acts" of the Great Story in this order. Nor do they have to hear the whole Great Story all at once. Most people at the thresholds of trust and curiosity may only be able to take in certain parts of the whole kerygma at one time. But in the end, an individual will need to be familiar with all the "Acts" and understand the kerygma as a whole before he or she can make a deliberate decision to follow Jesus as his disciple. Some people to whom we tell the Story will have been Catholic all their life but are not yet disciples, while some will not be baptized or have any Christian background at all. But all have the right to hear it. All need to hear it. But where we *begin* telling the Story can vary widely, depending upon our audience.

The Great Story of Jesus in Nine Acts

Act 1: The Kingdom
The version of the kerygma that I first heard as a funda-mentalist child in the Deep South began with "God loves

---

3   Johnson and Ross, *Atlas of Global Christianity: 1910–2010.*

you" and then segued immediately into "Here's your problem: you're a sinner." This can still work in the Bible Belt and in certain other settings.

My friend Barbara Elliott is founder of the Work-Faith Connection in Houston, which helps adults living in poverty or transitioning out of homelessness, prison, or unemployment to successfully reenter the workplace. Barbara points out that you don't have to convince most of the addicts and ex-cons going through the WorkFaith Connection that they are sinners. They already know it and are looking for redemption. But many in my hometown of Seattle would find the idea of "personal sin" both ridiculous and incomprehensible. When sharing the kerygma with a young Angelino or New Yorker who has been steeped in postmodern assumptions since birth, you are probably going to have to start in a very different place.

Jesus began his earthly ministry in his first-century Jewish context by proclaiming the Kingdom of God (see Matthew 4:17). What first-century Jews found compelling can also be surprisingly intriguing in the twenty-first-century West. Postmodern young adults who don't believe in personal sin are usually very aware of structural sin and therefore can find the idea of the Kingdom of God very attractive. That's why I have listed "The Kingdom" as the first "Act" of the Great Story. But again, this may not be the appropriate beginning place for everyone. Where you should start telling the Great Story depends upon the need and spiritual openness of the person with whom you are sharing. That's why I call the starting place "variable."

The proclamation of the Kingdom appeals to those who don't yet trust and those already at the thresholds of trust or early curiosity, just as it did to Jesus' first hearers. In that proclamation, we declare that God is love. He created us for a life with him full of love, peace, truth, beauty, goodness, and meaning that begins now, lasts forever, and can't be taken away. It is this life that Jesus preached and called the Kingdom or reign of God.

Act 2: Jesus, Face of the Kingdom

The life of the Kingdom can serve as a powerful "bridge of trust" to Jesus. The second act of our story is largely addressed to those at the threshold of curiosity. Jesus is not only the great prophet or announcer of the Kingdom — *he* is the presence of the Kingdom. The "kingdom shone out before men in the word, in the works, and in the presence of Christ."[4] An excellent biblical passage to share, which rouses curiosity, is this:

> And he came to Nazareth, where he had been brought up; and he went to the synagogue, as was his custom, on the sabbath day. And he stood up to read; and there was given to him the book of the prophet Isaiah. He opened the book and found the place where it was written,
>
> "The Spirit of the Lord is upon me,
> because he has anointed me to preach good news
> to the poor.

---

[4] *Lumen Gentium* (Dogmatic Constitution on the Church), 5 (online at www.vatican.va/archive/hist_councils/ii_vatican_council/documents/vat-ii_const_19641121_lumen-gentium_en.html, as May 8, 2012).

> He has sent me to proclaim release to the captives
> and recovering of sight to the blind,
> to set at liberty those who are oppressed,
> to proclaim the acceptable year of the Lord."
>
> And he closed the book, and gave it back to the
> attendant, and sat down; and the eyes of all in the
> synagogue were fixed on him. And he began to say
> to them, "Today this Scripture has been fulfilled in
> your hearing." (Luke 4:16–21)

If we help them encounter the actions and teachings of the Kingdom in the person of Jesus of Nazareth, people who are intrigued by the *Kingdom* can very easily become intrigued by Jesus the *man*. As evangelizers, we must always remember that "the kingdom of God is not a concept, a doctrine, or a program subject to free interpretation, but it is before all else a person with the face and name of Jesus of Nazareth, the image of the invisible God."[5]

Act 3: Jesus, the Kingdom in Word and Deed

Jesus is the face of the Kingdom, not only because he announces the Kingdom, but also because he does the works of the Kingdom. Jesus reveals the love of the Father and the nature of God's Kingdom through his every word and action. Jesus gives a frank answer to the messengers who come to him from John the Baptist, who is languishing in jail and struggling (as modern inquirers still do) with the question, "Are you he who is to come, or shall we look for another?" (Luke 7:20):

---

[5]   Pope John Paul II, *Redemptoris Missio*, 18.

In that hour he cured many of diseases and plagues and evil spirits, and on many that were blind he bestowed sight. And he answered them, "Go and tell John what you have seen and heard: the blind receive their sight, the lame walk, lepers are cleansed, and the deaf hear, the dead are raised up, the poor have good news preached to them. And blessed is he who takes no offense at me." (Luke 7:21–23)

Two deeds are particularly characteristic of Jesus' earthly ministry: healing and forgiving. These deeds signify that in the Kingdom there will no longer be sickness or suffering and that Jesus' mission is to transform people, free them from sin, and make them whole in body and spirit. He makes this particularly clear when he heals the paralytic:

When Jesus perceived their questionings, he answered them, "Why do you question in your hearts? Which is easier, to say, 'Your sins are forgiven you,' or to say, 'Rise and walk'? But that you may know that the Son of man has authority on earth to forgive sins" — he said to the man who was paralyzed — "I say to you, rise, take up your bed and go home." And immediately he rose before them, and took up that on which he lay, and went home, glorifying God. And amazement seized them all, and they glorified God and were filled with awe, saying, "We have seen strange things today." (Luke 5:22–26)

Jesus' healing miracles and authority to forgive sins raise the question of his divinity — "*Who is this?*" — which is naturally followed by another question, *"If Jesus is God, what does that mean?"* This is why there is no point in the New Testament at which Jesus is met with indifference or boredom. His presence always provokes either profound questioning or deep hostility. It drives those who are filled with honest curiosity toward and often across the threshold of openness to ponder the mystery of his passion.

Act 4: Jesus Embraces the Cross

At the threshold of openness, the inquirer is usually ready to face the fact that Jesus' ministry results not in "success" as the world understands it but rather in the mystery of his rejection, betrayal, crucifixion, and death. Yet it is *for us* that Jesus embraces the cross in obedience to the Father, as the means of our salvation and access to God's life. He himself testifies:

> For this reason the Father loves me, because I lay down my life, that I may take it again. No one takes it from me, but I lay it down of my own accord. I have power to lay it down, and I have power to take it again; this charge I have received from my Father. (John 10:17–18)

and

> The Son of man came not to be served but to serve, and to give his life as a ransom for many. (Matthew 20:28)

But the cross is not the end:

> He began to teach them that the Son of man must suffer many things, and be rejected by the elders

and the chief priests and the scribes, and be killed, and after three days rise again. (Mark 8:31)

Act 5: Resurrection, Ascension, New Life, Adoption, and the Kingdom

Confrontation with the biblical record of the resurrection of Jesus Christ is particularly meaningful for those at the thresholds of openness and seeking. The New Testament is absolutely clear: The entire Christian message stands or falls with the resurrection of Jesus Christ:

> If Christ has not been raised, then our preaching is in vain and your faith is in vain…. If Christ has not been raised, your faith is futile and you are still in your sins. Then those also who have fallen asleep in Christ have perished. If for this life only we have hoped in Christ, we are of all men most to be pitied. (1 Corinthians 15:14, 17–19)

The Resurrection is a historical event. Jesus appeared to many witnesses, and the New Testament and the tradition of the Church bear abundant witness not only to their testimony but also to the quality of their lives as honest witnesses to the risen Christ. Inquirers can study the historical evidence for the Resurrection and discover how powerful it is. Satisfied with that, they can then move on to the personal challenges of what the Resurrection means for each human person.

Because God has assumed our human nature, Jesus' life of perfect love and obedience, his death and resurrection *on our behalf,* break the bondage of sin and death. As the

Church teaches, "By His Incarnation, He, the Son of God, in a certain way, united himself with each man."[6]

Now, in his resurrection he opens the way to our own resurrection and to a new life for all: "For as in Adam all die, so also in Christ shall all be made alive" (1 Corinthians 15:22). Which takes us to the next act of the Great Story.

Act 6: Jesus Asks Me to Follow Him

To those standing at the thresholds of late openness and seeking, Jesus uses the same language he used with Simon and Andrew:

> As he walked by the Sea of Galilee, he saw two brothers, Simon who is called Peter and Andrew his brother, casting a net into the sea; for they were fishermen. And he said to them, "Follow me, and I will make you fishers of men." Immediately they left their nets and followed him. (Matthew 4:18–20)

The command to "follow" is one heard again and again in the Gospels. Jesus directs it not to everyone but to those who are truly seeking him. Sometimes he warns those who are not yet truly open or seeking that they need to count the cost. In short, his call to us is predicated on the reality that discipleship is not something that just "happens" but is a real decision and turning point requiring all the resources

---

[6] *Gaudium et Spes* (Pastoral Constitution on the Church in the Modern World), 22 (online at www.vatican.va/archive/hist_councils/ii_vatican_council/documents/vat-ii_cons_19651207_gaudium-et-spes_en.html, as of May 8, 2012).

of heart, mind, and strength we can muster — particularly since following Jesus involves that we obey, as Simon and Andrew did, his call to "repent, for the kingdom of heaven is at hand" (Matthew 4:17).

Act 7: Personal Sin and Forgiveness

The act of recognizing one's personal sin and need for forgiveness usually comes late in the journey of those who have absorbed the postmodern worldview. It can be difficult to grasp the reality of personal sin because it feels like an attack upon the self. As Scot McKnight observed about emerging adults (iGens):

> For a person to feel guilty, that person must have a sense of morality. But morality requires a potent sense of what is right and wrong, and it needs a powerful sense of what is true and false. Contemporary culture does not provide the average iGen with a profound grasp of what is right and wrong apart from the conviction that assaulting the self is clearly wrong.[7]

The Kingdom, with its prophetic revelation of structural sin, often functions as the twenty-first-century doorway into the reality of personal sin. As the *Catechism* points out, systemic sin is birthed, fueled, and sustained by the acts and sinful choices of individual people (CCC 1869), including us. The seeker must ultimately come to trust and seek Jesus enough to acknowledge what St. John the Apostle says: "If we say we have no sin, we deceive ourselves, and the truth is not in us" (1 John 1:8).

---

[7] McKnight, "The Gospel for iGens."

The forgiveness of sin — and therefore our need to acknowledge our sin — is at the heart of the Gospel: "Thus it is written, that the Christ should suffer and on the third day rise from the dead, and that repentance and forgiveness of sins should be preached in his name to all nations, beginning from Jerusalem" (Luke 24:46–47). And so we must face and repent of sin — *our personal sin*, which lies at the root of the great structures of systemic sin — since it was for the forgiveness of our personal sin that Christ suffered, died, and was raised from the dead.

Act 8: Dropping the Net

As the inquirer stands on the verge of discipleship, he is in the position that Peter was in when confronted by the challenge of who Jesus was:

> Jesus ... asked his disciples, "Who do men say that the Son of man is?" And they said, "Some say John the Baptist, others say Elijah, and others Jeremiah or one of the prophets." He said to them, "But who do you say that I am?" Simon Peter replied, "You are the Christ, the Son of the living God." And Jesus answered him, "Blessed are you, Simon Bar-Jona! For flesh and blood has not revealed this to you, but my Father who is in heaven." (Matthew 16:13–17)

As St. Paul says, "No one can say 'Jesus is Lord' except by the Holy Spirit" (1 Corinthians 12:3). The disciple cooperates with the Holy Spirit, making a conscious choice that requires faith in Jesus Christ as God, with the intention to follow him in what the Church calls the "obedience of faith." Discipleship is expressed by repentance of personal sin and baptism into Jesus' life, death, resurrection, and body on earth — the Church — or by the renewal of baptismal grace through confession and return to the regular practice of the faith.

Act 9: The Life of Discipleship

The new disciple is now ready to begin a lifetime of following Christ through the power of the Holy Spirit in the midst of his Church for the sake of the world. Newly baptized Sara Silberger speaks for many who have newly crossed into the world of relationship with God and discipleship:

> I wish that lifelong Christians, especially lifelong Catholics, could understand just for a minute what it is like to be lost. Maybe they would be less afraid to evangelize. It may be hard to explain…. Before I started this process, I thought of myself as a happy person, reasonably confident, proud of my life and how I lived it. It's not like I saw myself as stumbling around in a pit. But from where I stand now, wow.

> It was so different, so lonely. People talk about real Catholic discipleship as a lonely road — I do too sometimes — and it is frustrating, and stupid, and there is no good reason for it to be like that. But being without God is a different, deeper kind of being alone. I wouldn't even have known to call it lonely, because there isn't any concept that someone else should be there.

CHAPTER 11

Personally Encountering Jesus
in His Church

*For what profit is it to you, if Christ came once in the
flesh, unless he also comes into your soul?*

ORIGEN[1]

A fter breaking the silence, evangelizing parishes need to
look at how they can turn already existing ministries
into evangelization opportunities. Step 2 in creating a
culture of discipleship is to *create multiple, overlapping
opportunities for people to personally encounter Jesus in the
midst of his Church.* This can be

- through a relationship with a disciple;
- through Scripture: reading, study, *lectio divina*;
- through the teaching of the Church: formation,
  catechesis, religious education;
- through evangelizing, preaching, and teaching;
- through well-done, prayerful liturgy and music;
- through the sacraments;
- through a true inquiry process and evangelizing RCIA;

---

[1] Origen, *Homilies on Luke*, 22, 3, Joseph T. Lienhard, trans. (Washington,
DC: Catholic University Press, 1996), p. 94.

- through doing the works of Jesus, especially work with the poor and those who suffer;
- through encountering the real presence (Eucharistic Adoration);
- through personal prayer;
- through experiencing healing in Jesus' name;
- through evangelizing retreats and courses;
- through the discernment and exercise of the charisms;
- through hospitality: welcoming as though the stranger was Christ himself;
- through the experience of discipleship-centered Christian community;
- through beauty: the arts, music, architecture, media;
- through the lives and prayers of the saints;
- through devotions;
- through a good bookstore, book table, or library.

We need a wide spectrum of opportunities because there is no single silver bullet. We need to have a variety of different paths or doors to discipleship available and visible so that most people will find at least one way to connect with or draw closer to Christ. Instead of thinking of these ministries as separate, siloed endeavors run by different parish interest groups, we need to see all of our ministries in light of our primary call to make disciples. Armed with this vision and an understanding of the thresholds, we will begin to recognize amazing opportunities. We will realize that almost everything we do can be quite easily "reframed" for maximum evangelizing impact.

Craig Pohl and his team in Michigan are seeing some extraordinary fruit from doing just that:

We are continuing to run every program with one focus: bringing people into encounters with Jesus Christ, whether they have had an encounter before or never. Two years ago we restarted a Bible study for high school students. I started with six seniors: they gathered, studied, and prayed for more students to come. Now a quarter of the entire student body, 110 students, arrives voluntarily an hour before school starts. They read the Gospel, break up into groups, and talk about how the Scriptures are speaking to them. It is amazing!

We also held a prayer meeting with the Eucharist on the altar. It was explosive — praise and worship — then Father proclaimed the Gospel. The pastor took the Eucharist and walked through the crowd blessing people. We did find that people walked away more emboldened. We are going to start offering those prayer meetings once a month.

Using What God Has Given

There are a lot of potentially powerful evangelizing tools lying around the Kingdom workshop known as your parish. Initiatives like those in the following list are ideally suited to pre-evangelization. They can be occasions for building and restoring trust, fostering spiritual curiosity, and helping people become open to change:

- Inquiry
- Returning Catholics programs

- Faith formation/religious education (all ages)
- Small Christian communities of all kinds
- Social justice and service outreach to the larger community
- Liturgy: especially at Christmas and Easter, Advent and Lent, when many Catholics return
- Parish missions and other special evangelical and catechetical events (such as showing the *Catholicism* DVD series or bringing in a special speaker)
- Social events
- Pastoral counseling and spiritual direction
- Catholic schools
- Marriage preparation, support, and retreats
- Libraries and bookstores
- Websites, blogs, and social media

In addition, all parishes have structures in place that provide terrific opportunities for the proclamation of the kerygma. These include:

- RCIA;
- returning Catholics processes;
- liturgy/homily;
- faith formation/religious education (all ages);
- parish missions and other special evangelical/catechetical events;
- small Christian communities/study/prayer groups;
- evangelization training: how to share one's faith with others ;
- apologetics;
- parish-based evangelism retreats and experiences for the churched and unchurched (all ages);

- pastoral counseling, spiritual direction, reconciliation (confession).

For example, here's how things can change when the lens of discipleship gives us a whole new perspective on preaching, as it has for Dominican Father Mike Fones:

> My preaching has changed over the last few years. I am surprised by how often the Scriptures give me an opportunity to preach on conversion, on the meaning of the cross, on what it means to be a disciple of Jesus, and even on justification! Someone might say, "Well, that's just because you're looking at the Scriptures with that lens, that bias." I would counter with the possibility that, instead, my previous bias, which did not take life-changing conversion seriously, gave me "eyes that did not see" and "ears that did not hear" what I now see and hear so clearly.

Two resources in particular have dramatically changed the lives of millions of adult Catholics at the parish level: evangelization retreats or courses and RCIA. Let's begin by looking at evangelization retreats and processes in more detail.

Parish-based Evangelization Processes

Some well-known retreats and courses were created in particular parishes or regions, and then they spread from parish to parish, and even country to country. Some have been used for decades, and some are available in both Spanish and English. Here are a few retreats that have been used successfully for decades:

- Evangelization Retreats (Boise, Idaho)
- Light of the World (Rockford, Illinois)
- Christ Renews His Parish (Toledo, Ohio)
- Christian Experience Weekends (Iowa)
- Alpha for Catholics (Michigan)
- CaFE (Catholic Faith Exploration — Archdiocese of Westminster, London)
- Evangelizing Parish Cells (Florida)
- Life in the Spirit Seminar (global, Catholic charismatic renewal)[2]

All of these evangelization events are put on by lay people for lay people, with a priest acting as chaplain. Some, like the Evangelization Retreats, offer an opportunity for renewal of the sacraments of initiation (baptism, confirmation, Eucharist). The weekend retreats and multi-week courses usually include personal witness talks by lay people on pre-assigned topics, along with small-group discussion, meditation on Scripture, prayer, and adoration of the Blessed Sacrament. The topical witness talks are an excellent way to tell the Great Story of Jesus.

There are two main "streams" of evangelization experiences. Some, like Christ Renews His Parish and the

---

[2]   Visit the Catherine of Siena website at www.siena.org for more information on parish-based evangelization processes.

Christian Experience Weekend, are offshoots of the Cursillo Movement. Others emerged out of the charismatic renewal: Light of the World is a North American version of SINE (Sistema Integral de Evangelización), which originated in Mexico City. Word of mouth travels quickly, and effective retreats spread. For example, Alpha for Catholics is a Catholic adaptation of an evangelizing process that emerged from a charismatic Anglican church in London, while the Evangelizing Cells in Florida are an adaptation of a process first used in South Korea that later spread to Catholic parishes in Europe.

Inquirers and participants who attend Evangelization Retreats have almost always reached the threshold of trust: they attend the retreats because they trust a friend or family member who invited them. Some are already curious. Retreats can help people lower their defenses, declare themselves "open," and even move into seeking or discipleship in the course of a single weekend.

Christ Renews His Parish (CRHP) has had a big impact on St. John Fisher Parish in the archdiocese of Los Angeles over the past four years. Pastoral associate Katherine Coolidge is heavily involved in the retreat and the community that formed out of that experience:

> Christ Renews His Parish, with its 140 alumni, is beginning to have an impact. We had established a practice of fifteen minutes of prayer and reflection on the coming Sunday readings at parish meetings. When the CRHP alumni began to be called into parish leadership, the tenor of the "First 15," as we call it, was transformed. When CRHP alumni

joined our small-group network, they shared the power they were experiencing in a lived relationship with Christ. We have a committee dedicated to exploring what is a culture of discipleship, what are its implications, and how do we intentionally foster such a culture. We had a "mini" Making Disciples last month. Those who attended recognized the value in bringing in the Called & Gifted discernment process, which we are planning for next year. From there we need to investigate more entry points and venues in which people can consider a personal relationship with Christ.

Another friend, "Emily," is using a different multi-week evangelization process in her parish, where the percentage of intentional disciples is very low. Over two hundred people signed up for the first course! Even though the first experience was somewhat rocky, because most of the cradle Catholic facilitators didn't know how to respond to people asking serious spiritual questions, Emily witnessed lots of people moving from trust to curiosity, and even into seeking. One woman, a pillar of the community, revealed during the process that she didn't believe Jesus Christ was the Son of God, even though she goes to Mass every Sunday! This woman has now moved into spiritual curiosity. Emily also reports that several marriages have been healed.

Meanwhile "Ray," a parish leader in the Intermountain West, has created a four-week evangelization process that he just finished offering to fifty people, with very exciting results. In those four weeks, a number of participants crossed the frontier into intentional discipleship.

Caveat emptor: Not every process or source that calls itself "evangelizing" actually includes an explicit proclamation of the kerygma and challenges participants to "drop their nets." It is also important to know that most "evangelization" processes used in parishes (except Alpha and RCIA) were designed for practicing, marginal, or nonpracticing *Catholics*, not non-Christians or Christians from other traditions. The only parish-based process that we have encountered to date that routinely attracts large numbers of non-Catholics is the Evangelization Retreats in Boise. One-fourth of those participating are non-Catholic, many have spiritual breakthroughs, and some do become Catholic as a result.

THE EVANGELIZING RCIA

The other cornerstone of an evangelizing parish is a truly evangelizing RCIA process. "Ray" has not only created his own evangelizing course but also worked hard to transform his RCIA process into an evangelizing experience. When Ray took over leadership of RCIA, he invited the whole parish. "If you want to learn more about Jesus and his Church, come." They had about twenty-five attendees that first year: three were not Catholic; five were already disciples. During the inquiry phase, Ray and his team focused on evangelization and telling the Great Story of salvation. By the end of the first year, nine were disciples and the rest had moved into serious seeking. Ray writes:

> We are starting to see a huge spiritual hunger awaken. People didn't know that they didn't know.

Nobody had ever presented the Gospel to them in a way that was really clear. Once we did that, people began to respond. Our parish secretary had been here her whole life and on staff for ten years. In the past, she didn't attend Mass frequently; she said she attended "St. Mattress." But then she came to RCIA. From that moment, her heart and mind were open. Before that experience, no one had told her that she could have a personal relationship with God. She knew that there was rote prayer but that you could just talk to God and that He would respond was really new. Our RCIA is really drawing people into deeper intimacy with Christ and the Church. One cradle Catholic couple tells everybody, "RCIA changed our life."

Ideally, parishes should work toward having two or three different "reinforcing" evangelizing processes offered throughout the year. In a Florida parish, Evangelizing Cells, Eucharistic Adoration, and the Life in the Spirit Seminar make up the core of their annual cycle of evangelization. Sacred Heart Parish in Boise relies upon regular offerings of the Evangelization Retreats, Living in Christ mini-retreats, and the Called & Gifted discernment process as the central pieces of their parish evangelization plan.

USING THE THRESHOLDS IN PARISH EVANGELIZATION

Trained evangelization and RCIA team members can listen for beginning thresholds and recognize the journeys that participants make over the course of a retreat or program. I attended an Evangelization Retreat in Boise and was fascinated to witness the movement of one young woman in my small group from trust into openness, or possibly early seeking in the course of a single weekend. If you know that retreatants reached the end of the retreat in the thresholds of openness or seeking, your team can make sure they receive the kind of personal and spiritual support they need to continue the journey and flourish spiritually. Understanding the thresholds will also give you a much better sense of whether or not an inquirer is ready for the formal catechumenate, and if he or she possesses the necessary disposition to receive the sacraments of initiation fruitfully. Understanding the thresholds can also help team members evaluate the effectiveness of their efforts.

CHARISMS AS AIDS ON THE
JOURNEY TO INTENTIONAL DISCIPLESHIP

Charisms play a critical role in the mission of evangelization. Charisms are ways that you and I are empowered by God to be channels of his love, mercy, beauty, truth, wisdom, healing, and provision for others. The power of God flowing through a charism can help reveal Christ, remove impediments to belief, and encourage others to open their lives to God and receive sanctifying grace through the sacraments.

It is critical that we understand that charisms are given to all the baptized, not just to a few extraordinary Christians, and to individuals as well as to religious communities or movements. When it comes to making disciples, charisms really matter. We are not interchangeable cogs in an ecclesial machine. Being open to these gifts of the Holy Spirit, discerning them, and then exercising them for the sake of others are critical acts of obedience. God gives each of us particular charisms, so it really does matter that it is *you* and not someone else whom God has placed with *this* person.

After working with tens of thousands of Catholics in the discernment process, we have noticed something important: Not all charisms are welcomed and valued at the parish level. This is almost never intentional or bad-willed, but it hampers the work of the Kingdom all the same. For instance, the following charisms are typically welcomed and fostered in parochial settings:

- Administration
- Craftsmanship
- Encouragement
- Giving
- Helps
- Hospitality
- Mercy
- Music
- Pastoring
- Service
- Wisdom

Why are these charisms particularly welcomed? These are the spiritual gifts that are particularly useful in the liturgy, in caring for people, and when maintaining institutional structures. After doing many gifts interviews, I realized that there were typical gifts "profiles" for certain parish positions like youth minister, lay ecclesial minister, and even pastor. Most importantly, I came to realize which charisms were unusual in parochial ministry, and the practical problems that can arise when a parish leader has charisms that are out of the ordinary.

Which charisms are we not likely to welcome? *The charisms primarily aimed at starting new initiatives, evangelizing and proclaiming Christ, forming disciples and apostles, and freedom for unusual ministry and prophetic change.* Many of these gifts have been traditionally associated with religious communities rather than parish life:

- Celibacy
- Discernment of spirits
- Evangelism (except for youth ministry)
- Faith
- Healing
- Intercessory prayer
- Knowledge
- Leadership
- Missionary
- Prophecy
- Teaching
- Voluntary poverty
- Writing

These gifts are not usually highly prized within the average parish — yet. But God is bestowing a wide variety of charisms on his Church, and we need all the charisms he is sending! We can't afford to be unconsciously pushing away charisms that we don't see an obvious use for yet. If a charism is genuine,[3] then God has given it to people in our parish community for a reason. At this moment in our history, we particularly need the charisms ordered toward evangelization and making disciples. There is a real sense in which all the charisms contribute to forming a culture of discipleship. But certain gifts can be particularly helpful at certain thresholds of conversion. Here are a few examples.

People on the frontier of *trust* can be greatly encouraged by those with a gift of *hospitality*. The charism of hospitality empowers a Christian to be a generous channel of God's love by warmly welcoming and caring for those in need of food, shelter, and friendship. Such a charism can be used powerfully through work with the homeless or in your own home. The charism of hospitality could also be helpful when strategizing how to recognize and welcome those who are tip-toeing back in, perhaps in response to a Catholics Come Home television ad. Someone with a gift of hospitality would be critical on an RCIA team or the parish hospitality committee.

Similarly, spiritual *curiosity* is often evoked by the charism of *mercy*, which empowers a Christian to be a channel of God's love through practical deeds of compassion that relieve the distress of those who suffer and help them experience God's love. People with the charism of mercy tend to live lives that just do not make sense if God does not exist. They see the personal and spiritual beauty of those

---

[3]   Charisms must always be carefully discerned in the context of the Church. For more information about discernment, visit the Catherine of Siena Institute website at www.siena.org.

who suffer and feel privileged to serve them. And in the presence of one with the charism, suffering is dramatically eased and dignity restored. The charism can manifest fruitfully in work as a medical professional, a social or hospice worker, or as a Eucharistic minister to the sick. Christians with the charism of mercy become the face of the Kingdom and its King, and their very presence raises profound existential questions for the rest of us.

For those struggling with the anxiety-producing step of declaring oneself *open* to change, being around someone with a charism of *evangelism* can make all the difference. This gift empowers a Christian to share the faith with others in a way that draws them to become disciples of Jesus and responsible members of his Church. People with this charism are the ultimate contagious Christians. A Catholic with this charism will be regularly gauging where you and I are in our lived relationship with God. Are we drawing closer? Are we moving away? And they are praying about how to meet us where we are and help us move ever closer to Christ and his Church. Evangelizers with the charism don't have to manufacture opportunities to raise the topic of faith; it just seems to naturally come up when they are around. These people often spend their free time hanging out on the margins of the Church or beyond — wherever the spiritually seeking or wandering are to be found.

Unfortunately, the wonderful charism of evangelism makes most Catholics very uncomfortable. I call it the "stealth Catholic charism" because Catholics often try to hide the fact that a charism of evangelism is manifesting by calling it something more "respectable," like administration or teaching. In my experience, Catholics are more likely to be stunned (and sometimes horrified) by the discovery that God is using them in the area of evangelism than by the discovery of any other gift.

Those at the threshold of *seeking* may find those with gifts of *teaching* particularly helpful. Teaching empowers a Christian to be a channel of God's truth and wisdom, enabling others to learn information and skills that help them reach their fullest spiritual and personal potential. This is the person that you want to be giving initiatory catechesis in your RCIA or faith-formation offerings. Somehow, the subjects they teach — and they don't have to be religious in nature — seem vastly more interesting and compelling than we ever imagined. People with this charism make wonderful teachers — whether in a school, parish, or home setting — but also educational leaders and visionaries. They often become the creators of educational curricula.

Finally, those at the threshold of *intentional discipleship* can profoundly benefit from those with the charism of *pastoring*. To be installed as the canonical pastor of a parish, you have to be ordained. But you don't have to be ordained to exercise this intensely group-oriented charism, which is given widely to lay people and non-ordained religious. Pastoring empowers a Christian to be an effective channel of God's love through building Christian community by nurturing the relationships and long-term spiritual growth of a group. This is one gift that will be used entirely within the Christian community — even if it is a Bible study in the workplace.

Catholics with a charism of pastoring have an intense sense of what God will do when the Christian community is gathered together to pray or study or share faith. They are the geniuses of small groups. If small Christian communities don't exist in your parish when someone with this charism shows up, he or she will start them. The last thing that new disciples need is to feel isolated and alone within their parish. People with the charism of pastoring know that we were meant to find God and that we were meant to find him together.

Part of fostering a culture of discipleship is to expect conversion. If we expect God to transform lives, we need to have a plan so that our parishes encourage and support that transformation, rather than unwittingly suppress it.

CHAPTER 12

Expect Conversion

"Do you not say, 'There are yet four months, then comes the harvest'? I tell you, lift up your eyes, and see how the fields are already white for harvest."

JOHN 4:35

Several years ago a priest friend was talking to me about a woman he knew who had just gone through a conversion and was changing in dramatic ways. What astonished my friend was that the source of this woman's change wasn't catechetical. This new disciple was badly catechized, but the most astonishing spiritual wisdom was coming out of her mouth, and my priest friend couldn't get over it. What, he asked me, could be going on?

I sat for a moment in genuine bewilderment at his surprise. "Well ... it's the Holy Spirit," I said slowly. Surely, didn't this wonderful, intelligent, prayerful man understand what was happening? Didn't he know that manifestations of God's presence and significant — even dramatic — change are a common part of a new disciple's experience? It turned out that the answer was no. Even though he had been a priest for twelve years, my friend had never witnessed anyone go through a major conversion before.

One consequence of the lack of a culture of discipleship is that Catholics often don't expect to witness God at work.

We plan and work as though the mission of the Church depends entirely upon our hard work, cleverness, and institutions. When God's presence and power manifest in an obvious or dramatic fashion in a person or community, we often tend to back away.

For many centuries, the Church has taught that God gave us our intellect, will, and strength to use in his service. Catholicism famously honors the intellect in its relationship to faith. But we are seriously mistaken if we think and plan as though all we can expect to see happen in our parishes is what we could expect to see happen in any secular nonprofit filled with clever people. If we are going to seriously evangelize our own, we had better be prepared for the Holy Spirit to do things in people's lives and in our parishes that are not part of our five-year plans, things that we could never have accomplished even if they were part of our five-year plans. We have to *expect and plan for conversion and the fruit of conversion.*

How does one "plan" to cooperate with the work of the Holy Spirit? It is a fascinating and important question and one that few parishes are exploring. Certainly one important piece is to become clear about your basic Kingdom priorities.

KINGDOM PRIORITIES

In 2003, the Archdiocese of Los Angeles held a synod during which the New Evangelization was identified as the number one pastoral initiative. This gigantic archdiocese is broken into five regions. In 2009, Auxiliary Bishop Gerald

Wilkerson and the San Fernando region's evangelization committee and pastoral council adopted the following four pastoral priorities as their implementation strategy for the New Evangelization. In 2012, the archdiocese as a whole adopted these same four priorities:

1. To seek out and draw in the unbelieving and the unchurched.
2. To foster lifelong discipleship and spiritual growth.
3. To assist all the baptized in the discernment of their spiritual gifts (charisms) and vocations.
4. To equip and support extraordinary apostolates.[1]

Katherine Coolidge works as pastoral associate in a parish that lies in a different region of the archdiocese but was inspired by the San Fernando priorities. With the active support of their pastor, the parish evangelization committee and pastoral council identified seven key elements that are universal and need to be addressed by any parish community that desires to make disciples:

1. Prayer
2. Identifying the Unbelieving and the Unchurched
3. Sharing the Good News
4. Evangelizing: How and Where?
5. Forming and Equipping Disciples

---

[1] California Catholic Conference, "Grassroots Evangelization Formation Draws Hundreds in LA Archdiocese San Fernando Pastoral Region" (available online at www.cacatholic.org/index.php/issues2/education/168-grassroots-evangelization-formation-draws-hundreds-in-la-archdioceses-san-fernando-pastoral-region, as of May 8, 2012).

6. Transforming Society: Compassion and Mercy
7. The Financials

Katherine and her evangelization committee have developed some fabulous ideas that can be used by other parishes to stimulate prayer, discussion, and discernment among members of evangelization committees, pastoral councils, parish staff, and other interested parties. Of course, the specific action plan that this Los Angeles community came up with may not be appropriate in very different communities in other parts of the country. But all pastoral leaders can wrestle with these issues fruitfully:

* * *

1. Prayer
Ideas and proposals:

- Identify ways to invite existing prayer groups to pray for the ongoing work of evangelization in our parish.
- Provide opportunities for new prayer initiatives to form.
- Network prayer groups so that they support one another.
- Utilize technology and a prayer network to ask for the support of the intercessors in our community for the mission of the parish.
- Coordinate our efforts with existing and new efforts in the deanery, region, and archdiocese.
- The Eucharist, the source and summit of the Christian life, is our ultimate prayer.
    — How we evangelize should point toward and flow from our communal prayer and worship. And worship should make reference to the

work of disciples in the world, since the laity are called to offer all that they do in the world as spiritual sacrifices acceptable to the Father (see *Christifideles Laici,* 14).

— How we evangelize should point toward and flow from our communal prayer and worship.

— The celebration of our liturgy should reflect this vision of a body of evangelizing disciples.

— Offer ongoing formation and support to liturgical ministries, so that they live out this vision before, during, and after Mass.

2. Identifying the Unbelieving and Unchurched
Ideas and proposals:

• Develop ways to strategically identify those to whom we are sent: people in the community, occasional Mass attendees, and regular members of the parish.

• Develop a welcoming ministry in concert with this vision. Identify those with gifts, and provide them the formation, resources, and support to launch a comprehensive welcoming ministry, which may include
— parish partners,
— "welcome wagon" to all new residents within parish boundaries,
— newcomer gatherings.

3. Sharing the Good News
Ideas and proposals:

• Develop a sustainable, ongoing program by which parishioners can be formed and trained in the evangelization vision and skills offered in Making Disciples.

- Offer the small group, modulated version as well as the evening or day workshop option.
- Develop ongoing formation opportunities and meetings for those who complete the process in which to share stories and practice skills.
- Encourage all catechists — child, youth, adult, RCIA — to go through the training above.
- Incorporate modules of the training above into future parish evangelizing retreat teams formation.
- Explore the value of a Catholic Vacation Bible School as part of an evangelization strategy.
- Goal: Every person engaged in faith formation with any group able to share their own relationship with Christ.

4. Evangelizing: How and Where?
Ideas and proposals:

- Establish and communicate that our mission is to evangelize where we live: in the marketplace, in our homes, in the workplace, here at church.
- It is an expectation that our ministries and organizations are evangelizing.
- Ministry leaders and interested members should be offered an opportunity to complete Making Disciples.
- As part of any event planning, address how this event can evangelize. For example, how can we ensure individuals are present who are capable and competent at talking about their relationship with Christ? What follow-up evangelizing opportunities will be prominently advertised at these events?

- Ensure that some, if not all, of our Christian Life Communities offer the curious, open, and seeking opportunities to explore a lived relationship with Jesus in a safe, comfortable environment.
- In addition to Christ Renews His Parish, develop a half-day or one-day evangelizing retreat experience for those not ready or able to make a CRHP weekend.
- Provide opportunities for all interested parishioners to learn how to effectively evangelize one-on-one in the home, school, workplace, and marketplace.

5. Forming and Equipping Disciples
Ideas and Proposals:

(In Acts 9, a man named Ananias comes to Paul, who has been blinded by his encounter with Jesus on the road to Damascus. It was while Ananias was with Paul that he regained his sight and was baptized.)

- Offer a program to train and form "Ananiases," that is, spiritual companions to walk with and mentor new disciples.
- Develop discipleship small groups for support and ongoing formation.
- Provide opportunities for disciples to discern their giftedness and call from God (Called & Gifted workshops, discernment groups).
- Explore the support structure necessary for the ongoing support and formation of disciples. Does it already exist? Can existing leadership and administrative structures be tweaked to support ongoing discipleship training?

6. Transforming Society: Compassion and Mercy
Ideas and proposals:

- Explore how to communicate and connect the Gospel to what we do, re: outreach and pastoral-care ministries.

- Explore how we communicate to those we serve, that what we do is part of living out our call as a disciple of Jesus Christ.

- Offer spiritual and formation opportunities to those who serve so that they can see what they do as living out their call as a disciple of Jesus Christ.

- Provide spiritual formation for outreach-ministry members and leaders, such as retreats and mornings or days of reflection that allow them to see their service in light of their lived relationship with Jesus Christ.

- Provide the means and support to mission-focused groups as they explore, discern, and launch extraordinary apostolates.

- Consider how you might support disciples who are trying to live as such in their workplace — especially those who are really trying to be Christian bankers, lawyers, and so forth. It might be through small groups of professionals or talks given by them or with the pastor aimed at dealing with workplace issues. Finally, it might even come down to asking what concrete support you can give someone whose job is threatened if they do what their faith tells them to do. I think this will become more and more of an issue in the future. It's already a huge issue now in a post-Christian society such as ours.

7. Parish Resources
Ideas and proposals:

- Consult the wisdom of the finance council, as the development of evangelization strategy will have financial implications.
- Identify existing resources that already support this vision.
- Research and identify untapped resources in our community.
- Engage technology experts to explore how to reduce the maintenance burden so that more energy can be allocated to mission.
- All efforts include the collaborative efforts of staff and leadership councils dedicated to faith formation, stewardship, as well as evangelization.

* * *

Katherine touches upon one absolutely critical piece of the puzzle that we have recently recognized: How can we call forth and form "Ananiases," that is, spiritual companions to walk with and mentor new and renewed disciples? Because we have learned that in the absence of discipleship-centered Christian community, even the most independent and committed Catholics cannot flourish, and they begin to wither — and even leave.

THE POWER OF CHRISTIAN COMMUNITY

I have already talked about the isolation that can lead Catholics who are spiritual seekers to leave the Church. But what few people seem to understand is how debilitating spiritual isolation can be even for highly committed Catholics who are disciples. Many priests and lay leaders who are disciples and who long to evangelize experience a devastating isolation. At least half of the leaders who attended one Making Disciples seminar a few years ago expressed profound loneliness. They were from twenty-two dioceses all over the United States and Australia. They told us over and over again how isolated they were back home and how incredibly healing it was to be able to talk to other Catholics who cared about the same things they cared about. Just as discouraging was the fact that five deeply committed, orthodox Catholics had spontaneously used the same ominous language while talking with me during the two weeks prior to the seminar: "*If I left the Church....*" The reason for their despair was always the same: the lack of a community of spiritual friends with whom they could walk the path of discipleship.

I know that the idea of leaving the Church because you are grieving the fellowship of other disciples can be utterly mystifying or seem whiny and self-indulgent. How could you leave the Eucharist? Much depends upon whether or not you have ever experienced being part of a group of intentional disciples who were actively supporting one another. If you have, it can be extraordinarily difficult to live without it, for even the most committed.

David is a scholar and one of those deeply committed Catholics. He and his wife, Sherry, were members of our famously "Nameless" lay group in Seattle before they moved for the sake of David's career. This is how David describes his sense of spiritual isolation:

Friendships were key in Seattle. I want to be able to speak of what I truly hope for and the things that appear to thwart those hopes — and I could do that very easily in Seattle. People came to you for help and we did our best. It gave you a sense, when you participated in something like that, it was holy and this was what God wants us to be about.

Here I'm a father on my own with my wife and kids. So far, we've gotten by spiritually. God help us if we had a real crisis because there is nowhere to go here. I find that a hell of lot worse than not having insurance. I know what a true community "insurance" policy looks like, and I know what it can provide. It feels like I'm bleeding. How can you accept this? How can you expect so little of God?

Although David assures me that he would never leave the Church, I know a number of people who have. I also know many outstanding Catholic leaders who have told me privately that they are exhausted because they feel completely on their own, that they have no meaningful support in their parishes or dioceses except for their spiritual directors. And I am not just hearing it from the laity. I have yet to meet a pastor passionate about evangelization who hasn't told me privately that he feels almost completely alone in his concerns among his brother priests. One who is seeing lots of new disciples emerge in his parish vented recently:

Can I rant? It is amazing … the excuses and re-sistance to the Good News. You get some of these priests who say, "What are you smoking?" The older priests, we saw ourselves as men of the Church. *I* decide what that means, and it wasn't someone who had a personal relationship with Jesus. It was the wrong standard. If you want to leave a lasting impact on people's lives, it's not about your personality or your homilies. It is "have you helped them have a personal encounter with Jesus?" You are going to leave — but that lasts. It isn't about us. It is about the Lord.

This is not a uniquely twenty-first-century problem by any means. As Ralph Martin observes, St. Thomas Aquinas wrote over seven hundred years ago that the fruitfulness of the sacramental life is dependent upon the intentional support *of the community* as well as that of the spiritual life of the individual:

> The ongoing fruitfulness of a sacrament is tied to the quality of the "follow-up" or the environment of faith in which one lives, and the ongoing receptivity to the work of the Holy Spirit in the particular grace of the sacrament. Thomas acknowledges — even in his time — that the clergy are too busy to undertake this responsibility solely by themselves, but must involve the lay faithful in the task of follow-up.[2]

We know that the first year after one finishes RCIA or goes through a major conversion is critical and can be surprisingly difficult as the new disciple faces many unexpected obstacles and decisions. We also know that many converts

---

[2]   Martin, *The Post Christendom Sacramental Crisis.*

ultimately "drown" in the vast, lonely Catholic ocean. If we are serious about making disciples, we must intentionally support them once they are made. Most new disciples need an "Ananias," a disciple-companion, or an Ananias-like group of spiritual companions who understand what he or she is experiencing and will walk alongside.

As we make disciples in our congregations, some kinds of community will form naturally, but we will need to support spontaneous networks of friends with intentional discipleship-centered community building. How to do this is one of the Catherine of Siena Institute's highest priorities and something that many of our parish pioneers are experimenting with right now. Join us in prayer that our Lord receive the sacrifices of all those who have struggled with this, that many Ananiases will indeed be raised up to meet the challenges of the coming century. Which brings me to the critically important subject of the role of prayer in making disciples.

LAY THE SPIRITUAL FOUNDATION OF PRAYER

Resistance to spiritual culture change is to be expected and happens on many levels. This is why organized, sustained, corporate intercessory prayer for the spiritual renewal of our communities is essential. The charism of intercessory prayer empowers the intense prayer of a Christian for others to be the means by which God's love and deliverance reaches those in need.

Intercessory prayer is important for seekers at all stages, especially for those on the verge of openness and discipleship.

Sustained intercessory prayer for the spiritual renewal of one's parish can change the spiritual atmosphere of a place and increase the frequency of external and internal actual graces. Corporate intercession can greatly increase the spiritual openness of individuals — even those who just "drop in" — and break the power of spiritual bondages that oppose the purposes of God. Parish leaders who are serious about making disciples are discovering how critical it is to deal with spiritual opposition through prayer. One of them recently wrote me about their experience of the power of prayer:

> There was real spiritual oppression going on here. Members of parish staff were involved in the occult. When you would speak to a group or the pastor would give a homily, it just felt like there was a wall or black hole — the words were just sucked down. Whatever was being shared didn't go anywhere — like the seed falling on rocky ground. No one had ever talked to them about the Gospel. Now, that wall is gone. A lot of that is because of our intercessory prayer group. Our spiritual climate has changed; people are responding and asking for more. Young families are moving into our parish because they had heard that something is going on here.

We have also seen that astonishing things can happen through prayer in the lives of those on a spiritual quest. A friend who is leading a seeker group shared this story:

> They were praying the whole week before our session for the grace to experience Jesus' personal love

so that we might grow in trusting him more. I believe these graces are playing into the session greatly. Some of the participants begin to share how they are afraid to trust Jesus.

One woman shared her experience. She said that her son, who is sixteen, went to a theme park and was supposed to be home at 2:00 A.M. He didn't show up on time, and she began to feel so worried about him.

The next day as she prayed, she asked Jesus for the grace [to experience Jesus' desire for a personal relationship], and it came to her that her longing for her son to come home was how Jesus feels about her. He is longing for her to come home to him.

Another man shared that after praying he got into bed and closed his eyes when suddenly he felt someone enter the room, walk toward the bed, lean over him, and kiss him on his forehead. He said he felt so much love, love like he had never felt before. He said he couldn't sleep that night but felt so loved that he just had to journal about the experience.

Where does that leave us? The infinitely good news is that God has made provision for all our weaknesses and needs, and for our mission of evangelization. But like discipleship, obtaining this provision requires that we embark on a spiritual quest. Much of God's provision comes to us in response to the sustained prayer of his Church as she prepares to run the race of discipleship in a given time and place.

MISSION, COMMUNITY, AND THE LEADVILLE EFFECT

Every August, hundreds of outsiders descend on Leadville, Colorado, to attempt the highest ultra-marathon in North America: the Leadville Trail 100, "The Race Across the Sky." Competitors run or walk one hundred miles across terrain that rises as high as 12,600 feet. The race begins at 4:00 A.M. on Saturday. You have to stagger across the finish line before the gun goes off at 10:00 A.M. on Sunday. To finish on time, runners cannot sleep, and they must run or walk, all day and night, up and down steep, icy mountain trails. This past August, 347 runners finished. Six finishers were in their sixties.

Everyone thinks it is crazy — until you witness a race. Then what I have come to think of as the "Leadville Effect" hits you. What do I mean?

The Leadville Effect is what happens when "ordinary" people begin to imagine, aspire to, and then accomplish extraordinary things because their community intentionally supports outstanding achievement. What's the secret? *No one runs alone.* Finishing Leadville is not about youth and speed. Finishing Leadville is about courage and heart and the power of community.

There is a minimum of two volunteers for every runner. Aid stations operate all day and night, handing out water, Gatorade, power gels, cookies, and hot potato soup. Volunteers time runners in and out of aid stations, weigh them, assess their conditions, give them chances to warm themselves and change their clothing and gear, and if necessary, stop them before they hurt themselves.

In addition, most runners have their own personal teams of supporters. Many have "pacers" who run beside them for as much as fifty miles. Throughout the night, pacers can be heard softly encouraging, challenging, and making sure their runners keep hydrated and don't get lost. Family and friends, wearing matching sweatshirts, with mottos like "Ted's team," meet the runners at aid stations with specially prepared food, changes of clothing, and sunblock. They massage and bandage battered feet and provide dry shoes and socks — and a stream of encouragement.

The whole drama culminates at the finish line between 9:00 and 10:00 A.M. on Sunday morning. A few years ago I could not help but notice a large support team of perhaps forty people, all dressed in scarlet T-shirts, near the finish line. I asked a couple of the team members which runner they were supporting. They pointed to the front of their shirts, which read, "In loving memory of Greg." Twenty-five-year-old Greg had drowned in a river the summer before. His wife, "Beth," was running the Leadville 100 in his memory. A few minutes later word spread among the team that Beth was two miles away, with only an hour of race time remaining. Instantly her army set off to meet her.

I waited by the finish line. One by one runners crossed, many running hand-in-hand for the last hundred yards with the spouses, children, and friends who had made their achievement possible. Grizzled men broke down and wept in joy and relief within seconds of finishing. But I kept my eye on the ridge of the last hill, looking for signs of Beth.

Then I saw it: A scarlet phalanx formed on the crest of the hill and began marching steadily toward us. As the group drew closer, I could see that they had formed a cheering, human wall around a young woman with long brown hair. Beth's pacer was beside her. Her friends were carrying all her gear, freeing her up to focus on one thing alone: finishing. Beth was limping, but her face was radiant as she crossed the line eighteen minutes before the final gun went off.

The power of that experience has stayed with me because it has such obvious implications for the formation of Catholic disciples and apostles. I know many "Beths," women and men who are doing astonishing things for the Kingdom of God only because they have the active, sustained, enthusiastic support of the Christian community — an ecclesial Leadville Effect. In the end, the Catholic understanding of salvation is incorrigibly communal. We are all in this together, because none of us are saved by ourselves alone: we are saved as members of the Church, the body of Christ. The hand cannot say to the foot, "I do not need you."

THE WEIGHT OF GLORY

It should not surprise us that a parish-wide culture of intentional discipleship is built and reinforced by the love, charisms, prayer, sacrifices, energy, and discipleship of *many* people, not just pastors and staff and "officially" recognized leaders. In order to evangelize our own within the Church and those whose lives we touch outside, we need to deliberately form a *wide* range of Catholic disciples to

- ask where people are in their relationship with God;
- listen well, respectfully, and prayerfully;
- recognize spiritual thresholds in one another;
- respond helpfully to one another's current spiritual needs;

- articulate the basics of the Great Story in a way that invites intentional discipleship;
- challenge one another to make the decision to follow Jesus as a disciple;
- celebrate and support intentional discipleship.

There is great cause for hope. The Holy Spirit has our back; he is creating a vast community of love in which, slowly but surely, we are learning the steps of the Great Dance of the Blessed Trinity. Jesus promises to be with us always, even to the end of the world. And because of this we can trust that he will give his Church what is necessary in this hour, as in all hours past, to meet the challenge of this time. We can, in a word, pray for and expect conversion. As C. S. Lewis wrote:

It may be possible for each to think too much of his own potential glory hereafter; it is hardly possible for him to think too often or too deeply about that of his neighbor. The load, or weight, or burden of my neighbor's glory should be laid on my back, a load so heavy that only humility can carry it, and the backs of the proud will be broken.[3]

May God grant us the humility to carry the weight of our neighbor's glory in the twenty-first century and ultimately into eternity, through Christ our Lord.

---

[3]   C. S. Lewis, *The Weight of Glory*, New York: Macmillan Publishing, 1980, p. 18.

About the Author

Sherry Weddell co-founded the Catherine of Siena Institute with Father Michael Sweeney, O.P., to equip parishes to form lay Catholics for their mission in the world. Sherry created the first gifts-discernment program designed especially for Catholics, and she currently leads CSI's international team of teachers and facilitators, who have formed over 85,000 lay, religious, and ordained Catholics in 105 dioceses in the art of evangelizing postmoderns, in gifts and vocational discernment, and in understanding the theology and mission of the laity. When not on the road, Sherry and her husband enjoy the challenge of turning a Rocky Mountain "fixer-upper" into a Tuscan villa and garden.